The Bells of Nagasaki

The ruins of Urakami Cathedral. Makoto (14) and Kayano (8) in front of the statue of the Grieving Virgin, January 1948.

The Bells of Nagasaki

Takashi Nagai

Translated by William Johnston

KODANSHA INTERNATIONAL
Tokyo, New York & San Francisco

Publication of this translation was assisted by a grant from the Japan Foundation. Photographs were lent by Chuo Shuppan and Makoto Nagai.

Originally published in 1949 by Hibiya Shuppan under the title *Nagasaki no kane*.

Distributed in the United States by Kodansha International/USA Ltd., through Harper & Row, Publishers, Inc., 10 East 53rd Street, New York, New York 10022. Published by Kodansha International Ltd., 12–21, Otowa 2-chome, Bunkyo-ku, Tokyo 112 and Kodansha International/USA Ltd., with offices at 10 East 53rd Street, New York, New York 10022 and the Hearst Building, 5 Third Street, Suite No. 430, San Francisco, California 94103. Copyright © 1984 by Kodansha International Ltd. All rights reserved. Printed in Japan.
LCC 84-47686
ISBN 0-87011-617-7
ISBN 4-7700-1117-2 (in Japan)
First edition, 1984

INTRODUCTION
by William Johnston

On Thursday, August 9, 1945, at two minutes past eleven in the morning, the Urakami district of Nagasaki was wiped out by a plutonium atomic bomb which exploded at a height of some five hundred meters over the city.

Among the wounded on that fateful day was Dr. Takashi Nagai, nuclear physicist, dean of the radiology department in the medical school of the University of Nagasaki and (since in wartime he had a military title) head of the Eleventh Medical Corps. Swept into the air by the atomic blast (he himself describes it graphically) and buried beneath a heap of rubble and broken glass, he managed to extricate himself from the mess and gathered together a little band of doctors, students, and nurses who devoted themselves with indefatigable zeal to the service of the sick and dying.

After three days of sweat and toil, the wounded Nagai made his way home. His house was burned to the ground and his beloved wife, Midori, was dead. So he picked up her charred bones and carried them to a relief center in the countryside where he and his team continued to dedicate themselves with heroic selflessness to the wounded and dying. And as they devoted themselves to the sick, this little group of people was profoundly conscious of its vocation not only as rescue workers but also as students and scholars of a university. They knew they faced a situation that was unique in the annals of medical history; and with eyes fixed on the future of medicine they assiduously studied the effects of the bomb on their own bodies and on the bodies of those they tended.

But it soon became clear that the heroic rescuers were just as sick as the wounded they served. One by one they collapsed, and after a month Nagai himself became critically ill. Before the bomb fell he had already contracted leukemia—probably the result of his dangerous radiology research. And now his right carotid artery was cut when one side of his body was pierced by pieces of flying glass. The loss of blood and lack of food and sleep were too much for his overworked body, and on September 26 he fell into a coma and came to the brink of death.

How he recovered is a mystery. But recover he did; and after submitting a scientific report to the university he wrote *The Bells of Nagasaki*. The book was completed in August 1946, exactly one year after the atomic explosions.

The book is not scholarly (though the author uses enough technical terms to give severe headaches to the uninitiated translator), nor is it merely popular. It is an eyewitness account of a terrible event in human history; it is the heroic story of a small group of doctors, nurses, and students; it is a poignant cry for world peace. Nevertheless, it seems to have come under the category of subversive literature, for the Occupation authorities of General Douglas MacArthur refused permission for its publication. If this seems strange, let the reader consider the historical background. This was a time when the International Military Tribunal of the Far East, which sat in Tokyo from May 1946 to November 1948, was sentencing Japanese war leaders to death or imprisonment. In these circumstances it is understandable that the victors were reluctant to be reminded of their own war crimes. At any rate, permission to publish was refused.

Undaunted by this rebuff, however, the friends of Nagai appealed to Washington, where the Department of Defense finally gave permission for publication—with the proviso that an appendix be added describing Japanese atrocities in the Philippines. This was promptly done. But the red tape devoured time; and Nagai did not see his book in print until January 1949.

It quickly became a best seller and was made into a movie with a popular song which I heard all around me when I first came to Japan in 1951. The book never went out of print (though the appendix about Japanese atrocities in the Philippines was duly omitted when the American Occupation ended) and it is widely read to this very day.

But let me say something more about the early Nagai.

He was born in Matsue on the Japan Sea in 1908. His father was a doctor and young Takashi, following in the paternal footsteps, entered the medical school of the University of Nagasaki. After graduation he remained in the university as a lecturer, at the same time serving as a medical corpsman. In 1931, we find him with the Japanese army in the so-called Manchurian Incident and again in 1932, in the Shanghai Incident. In 1940, he became assistant professor of radiology; and when the atomic drama opens in 1945, he is already dean of the department. Since most of the young men

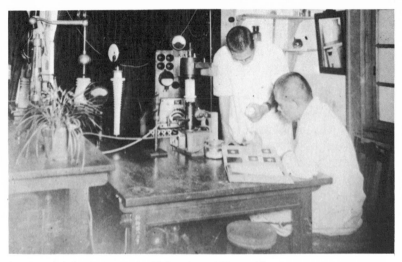

A research laboratory at the University of Nagasaki.

were at the front, responsibility for the whole department fell heavily on his shoulders.

A deeply religious person, he has written that (like many Japanese intellectuals of his time) he was greatly influenced by the *Pensées* of Pascal. Yet another influence on his religious life was the cathedral bells—echoing and reechoing across the valley and calling him to prayer. Those bells survived the atomic blast and can still be seen in the Atom Bomb Museum in Nagasaki.

But the chief influence in his religious life was neither Pascal nor the cathedral bells. Far greater than these was the influence of the woman he loved. It was Midori Moriyama, a Nagasaki Christian and a child of martyrs, who led him to faith. They were married in 1934, and had two charming children, Makoto and Kayano, who figure prominently in his books as children of the atom bomb and children of the new age.

Nagai was a patriot. He was also an intellectual. He knew what was happening in the world of politics and the world of science. He knew that American scientists were working on an atomic bomb. He knew that the "Big Three" had issued a proclamation from Potsdam. For a better understanding of his book, then, let me say a word about the historical background to that savage and complex world of 1945.

On July 15, 1945, the Big Three—Harry S. Truman, Joseph Stalin, and Winston Churchill—met at Potsdam near the ruined city of Berlin to discuss the future of the postwar world. By now it was clear that the Japanese Empire had crumbled and that the Second World War was crashing to a close. Germany was defeated. Russia was preparing to declare war on an isolated and friendless Japan. American forces, having captured island after island in the Pacific, were firmly entrenched in the Marianas, in Iwo Jima, and in Okinawa—and flushed with victory they were turning triumphant eyes toward the Japanese mainland. The Japanese air force and navy were crippled. Thousands of tons of bombs had rained on Japanese cities. Fire bombs on Tokyo on March 10 had killed 140,000 people, and on May 26 a similar great devastation had taken place. In Japan, food was short; raw material was short; transportation was breaking down. It was clear that the end was in sight.

And the Japanese government was aware of its awful predicament. A message signed by Foreign Minister Togo was sent to Ambassador Sato in Moscow telling him to call immediately on Molotov, before the Russians set out for Potsdam, and to explain to him the emperor's earnest desire to bring hostilities to an end. The message was intercepted and decoded by American intelligence: Washington knew exactly what was happening.

And then at Potsdam, on July 16, Truman received the earth-shaking news he had eagerly awaited: an atomic bomb had been successfully tested at Alamogordo in New Mexico. The billion-dollar Manhattan Project had achieved its aim. The work of the brilliant Robert Oppenheimer and his colleagues at Los Alamos had been crowned with success. "The most secret and the most daring enterprise of the war had succeeded," wrote Truman later. "We were now in possession of a weapon that would not only revolutionize war but could alter the course of history and civilization."[1]

The triumphant Truman, together with Winston Churchill and Chiang Kai-shek, now issued the epoch-making Potsdam Declaration calling for unconditional surrender from Japan. The concluding clause ran as follows:

> We call upon the government of Japan to proclaim now the unconditional surrender of all Japanese armed forces, and to provide proper and adequate assurances of their good faith in such action. The alternative for Japan is prompt and utter destruction.

The proclamation made no mention of the atomic bomb.

The next act in this extraordinary drama is filled with confusion and misunderstanding. In Japan, Prime Minister Suzuki, after consultation with his cabinet, told the press that the proclamation was unimportant and they must *mokusatsu* it. The word literally means "to kill with silence," and Suzuki later claimed that he had no intention of rejecting the proclamation and that the best English translation of his words would be "No comment." But in the West, the word was interpreted as contemptuous rejection.

And the rejection of the Potsdam Declaration was the alleged reason for the dropping of the first atomic bomb.

The decision to drop the atomic bomb, one of the most awesome decisions in world history, has been the subject of endless controversy involving some of the central figures in the annals of the twentieth century. The actual decision was made by Harry Truman, who seemingly never regretted it. Dwight Eisenhower, who was at Potsdam (though not present at the meeting of the Big Three), vehemently opposed the bomb saying that Japan was already defeated, that the bomb was totally unnecessary, and that he hated to see the U.S. initiate the use of something so horrible and destructive.[2] Bertrand Russell, after the event, called Hiroshima "a wanton act of mass murder." The Catholic Church, again after the event, stated solemnly that "any act of war aimed indiscriminately at the destruction of entire cities . . . is a crime against God and humanity itself."[3]

Most fascinating, however, was the dramatic struggle within the scientific community. The scientists alone were in the know (for the secret was carefully guarded) and as they toiled to make the bomb they were not without ethical and religious scruples.

The whole story begins in 1939, when Albert Einstein, encouraged by the distinguished physicist Leo Szilard, wrote a letter to Roosevelt recommending the development of atomic energy for military purposes. At that time it was rumored that Nazi Germany was working with nuclear energy and it seemed that whoever got the bomb first would win the war. And so in the early 1940s it was thought that scientists in Germany and the U.S. were in a neck-and-neck race.

When Germany was defeated, however, Einstein and Szilard had grave doubts about the wisdom of using an atomic bomb against Japan. And a second letter from Einstein, this time deprecating the use of the bomb, was found unopened in Roosevelt's mail in Warm Springs, Georgia, at the time of his death in April 1945.

But now the scientific community was divided. Truman had established an "Interim Committee" of experts under the chairmanship of Secretary of War Henry Stimson and assisted by a group of atomic scientists including Robert Oppenheimer, Arthur H. Compton, E. O. Lawrence, and Enrico Fermi. Truman later wrote that the members of this committee recommended that the bomb be used as soon as possible. "They recommended further," he goes on, "that the bomb be used without specific warning and against a target that would clearly show its devastating strength."[4] But Leo Szilard, with the backing of Einstein, continued to campaign against the bomb and was one of sixty-three scientists who sent a petition to Truman asking him not to approve military use of the bomb against the cities of Japan.

Objections to the bomb were not just humanitarian. It was not just the horrible destruction and the appalling loss of life that bothered the scientists. Some of them were already looking into the future. They saw that humanity was entering a new era. If the bomb was once used, where would it end? Six days before the test explosion in New Mexico, a committee composed of eminent physicists and chemists under the chairmanship of Dr. James Franck sent a report (known as the *Franck Report*) to Secretary of War Stimson in which they said:

> Unless an effective international control of nuclear explosives is instituted, a race for nuclear armaments is certain to ensue. . . . Within ten years other countries may have nuclear bombs. . . . We believe that these considerations make the

use of nuclear bombs for an early unannounced attack against Japan inadvisable. If the United States were to be the first to release this new means of indiscriminate destruction upon mankind, she would sacrifice public support throughout the world, precipitate the race for armaments, and prejudice the possibility of reaching an international agreement on the future control of such weapons.[5]

This is prophetic. The scientists saw the awesome responsibility of their country. If the United States used the bomb, others would follow. If the United States refrained from using the bomb, it might be banned forever. In short, these scientists foresaw the arms race and the awful predicament in which we find ourselves today.

Moreover, there was an unmistakably religious dimension to the anxiety of some scientists. Laura, wife of Enrico Fermi, has written that among the Los Alamos scientists there was a "sense of guilt." And Oppenheimer himself was to say that "in some crude sense which no vulgarity, no humor, no overstatement can quite extinguish, the physicists have known sin; and this is knowledge which they cannot lose."[6] Indeed, Oppenheimer never lost this sense of sin and as he grew older he became more committed to peace.

Now, from all I have said one might conclude that there was a lot of political controversy and soul-searching before the bomb was dropped. But surprisingly Winston Churchill states categorically that this was not so. He claims that at Potsdam there was never a moment's discussion as to whether the atomic bomb should be used or not. It was perfectly obvious to all that it should be used. "There was unanimous, automatic, unquestioned agreement around our table; nor did I ever hear the slightest suggestion that we should do otherwise."[7]

How does one explain this paradox? Was it that the objections of the scientists never reached the ears of Truman? I prefer another explanation.

While Truman took full responsibility for the decision, there was a sense in which he did not make it. He was carried along by the tide of events. Two billion dollars had been spent on the atom bomb project, years of research had gone into it; many people were working with the assumption that the bomb would be used. Churchill took it for granted. Stalin, hearing about the new weapon, expressed the hope that Truman would make good use of it against the Japanese. There was the additional fact that the collective unconscious of the time, conditioned by years of war, was thirsty for blood, clamoring for revenge, impatient to see the end. Only by a heroic act of will running counter to the spirit of the times could Truman have stopped the dropping of that bomb. In a certain sense he was the pawn, the instrument, the victim.

Truman and his advisors chose four cities as targets. In order of importance they were: Hiroshima, Kokura, Niigata, and Nagasaki.

And so the giant B-29 *Enola Gay* (named after the mother of Colonel Tibbets who led the operation) set out from the Pacific island of Tinian carrying a uranium atomic bomb nicknamed "Little Boy." It was three and a half meters long and sixty centimeters in diameter. And on August 6, at 8:15 A.M., it parachuted down and exploded in the clear sky over Hiroshima at a height of approximately five hundred meters from the ground.

How many people died? "That day," writes John Toland, "perhaps 100,000 human beings perished in Hiroshima, and an equal number were dying from burns, injuries, and a disease of the atomic age, radiation poisoning."[8] He goes on to quote Professor Shogo Nagaoka of the Peace Memorial Museum in Hiroshima to the effect that at least two hundred thousand died as a result of the bomb.

Meanwhile Truman, still in Potsdam, received a message from Henry Stimson, secretary of war, which read:

Big bomb dropped on Hiroshima August 5 at 7:15 P.M. Washington time. First reports indicate complete success which was even more conspicuous than earlier test.

Truman, the historians tell us, greeted the news with evident satisfaction. "We have gambled two billion dollars and won," he was to say later. He now held the trump card against Japan—and against Russia.

A few days later a B-29 carrying the second bomb set out again from Tinian. The plane was called *Bock's Car* and was piloted by Major Charles Sweeney, who had been in one of the planes that flew over Hiroshima, with Captain Ashworth as copilot. The bomb was a spherical plutonium missile, nearly four meters long and almost two meters in diameter called the "Fat Man" in honor of Winston Churchill. Two other B-29s followed closely behind mounted with highly sensitive cameras to record the destruction of the city. And at two minutes past eleven in the morning of August 9, the bomb exploded at a height of about five hundred meters.

What happened on the ground is adequately described by Takashi Nagai. Here let me simply quote the statistics I found in the Peace Memorial Park in Nagasaki:

Dead: 73,884
Injured: 74,909
Sufferers: 120,820
Houses burned down: 11,574
Houses half-ruined: 5,509
Houses partly damaged: 50,000

The Interim Committee had asked that the bomb be used without specific warning and against a target that would clearly show its devastating strength. The dying Nagai prayed: "Grant that Nagasaki may be the last atomic wilderness in the history of the world."

Meanwhile *Bock's Car* returned to its base and the crew was greeted with the news that Russia had entered the war in the Far

East. Ambassador Sato had finally met Molotov, only to be greeted with a declaration of war. And immediately Soviet troops began a massive invasion of Manchuria.

As for the survivors in Nagasaki, they heard the voice of their emperor announcing the end of the war: ". . . The enemy has begun to employ a new and most cruel bomb, the power of which to do damage is indeed incalculable. . . . Should we continue to fight, it would . . . result in the ultimate collapse and obliteration of the Japanese nation. . . ." He never made a truer speech. Two more atomic bombs were ready on Tinian and tentative plans had been made for drops on August 13 and 16. Tokyo was a possible target.

At this time Nagai and his heroic team of rescuers were tending the wounded at their relief center in the mountains. And one of their number returned from the city with the devastating news.

While telling the story of the Nagasaki bomb, Nagai unconsciously tells his own story. It is a story of conversion and transformation—a conversion and transformation that have been effected through intense suffering. He has lost everything. He has lost his beloved wife, his house, his possessions, his health. He has seen his people by the thousands torn and lacerated by atomic wounds. He has seen the destruction of the Japanese cities, the collapse of the Japan he loved, the failure of the ideology to which he dedicated his life. He has seen the cruel humiliation of his country, culminating in the surrender on the battleship *Missouri* and the American Occupation of Japan. And now he lies dying, knowing that his children will be orphans.

And through this suffering a new and prophetic Nagai is born. Previously he was passionately devoted to the sick as part of the Japanese war effort; now he is passionately devoted to the sick because they are human beings. Previously he was devoted to victory for Japan; now he is devoted to world peace. He still loves his country; but now he is committed to the spiritual reconstruction of a Japan that will work for world peace. His whole life is centered on the greatest commandment, the commandment of love.

From the relief center in the mountains, he moves to a tiny hut built on the site of his former house, the house in which Midori died in the atomic blast. It is called "Nyokodo," meaning "Love-Your-Neighbor-as-Yourself House" and represented by the Japanese characters:

His little hut has been preserved and is now a place of pilgrimage. It reminds one of Gandhi's tiny room in New Delhi. Like the Mahatma, Nagai wanted to live among the poorest of the poor and to possess nothing.

And here he meditates. "In order to find a way I sit thinking and meditating," he says to his young visitors. "But as yet I have found no answer." And then he vigorously gives them advice:

> "Go to the mountains and meditate! If you stay in the hurly-burly of this world, you'll run around in circles without ever finding your way. You'll become the kind of person who just stamps and screams. But the blue mountains are immovable and the white clouds come and go. I look constantly at these three mountains of Mitsuyama and continue my meditation."

And through suffering and through meditation he does find an answer.

Midori, the author's wife.

His message is simple: Love your neighbor as yourself. This is the way, the only way, to world peace. And living this message he takes an honored place among the great prophets of Asia and of the world. As a prophet of peace and love with a unique experience he stands beside Mahatma Gandhi, Martin Luther King, Dorothy Day, Thomas Merton, and the other great lovers of peace in our century.

Rich indeed was his transformation. This professor who before 1945 had written nothing but scholarly reports with dry statistics now becomes a writer, a poet, an artist, a humanist, a mystic. Lying on his sickbed with his writing pad suspended over his head, he writes no less than twenty books before his death in 1951. He also writes poetry. Though Japanese poetry does not translate well into English let me refer to one.

The girls of Junshin School died in the atomic blast chanting psalms under the leadership of one of their Japanese nuns, just as

the twenty-six martyrs of Nagasaki had died centuries before on
crosses chanting psalms under the leadership of Paul Miki. About
these schoolgirls Nagai wrote:

> Virgins like lilies white
> Disappeared burning red
> In the flames of the holocaust
> Chanting psalms
> To the Lord.

Nagai was also a master of calligraphy. As love for peace became
an all-consuming passion he would write for his visitors the
characters *heiwa wo*, meaning "Grant us peace!" Here are his own
inimitable characters:

A thousand copies of these characters have been preserved.

When he could no longer write he painted watercolors depict-
ing the mysteries of Christ's life and death. And when the end drew
near and he could no longer hold a brush he recited the rosary (the
dead Midori was found clutching the rosary beads in her right
hand), praying after each decade: *Heiwa wo*—Grant us peace!

And so Nagai the scientist, Nagai the patriot, Nagai the humanist
becomes Nagai the mystic. He is a mystic of peace for our times.

In the vast quantity of atomic literature and art, the work of Nagai has a unique place. For he is not only an eyewitness who graphically describes what happened: he is also a thinker who attempts a theology born of cruel suffering and painful conversion of heart.

The basis of his theology is faith. That the bomb fell on Nagasaki was no accident. That the bomb exploded over the cathedral was no accident. All this was somehow planned by a loving God and it all has meaning.

But his main theological insight concerns the value of suffering. The atomic bomb has maimed and mutilated thousands of bodies but it has not broken the spirit of Nagai and his companions. It has transformed them. It has made them heroes. Wounded and dying, they are filled with that paradoxical joy that comes from love—and in the midst of their suffering they break out in flashes of genuine humor.

And for Nagai, suffering has value not only for the transformation of the human person but also for the redemption of the world. Those who died in the atomic holocaust (particularly those who died while praying in the cathedral) were lambs offered to God in reparation for the sins of the Second World War. There had to be a death; there had to be an atonement. And the dead in Nagasaki were chosen for this role and this mission. Thanks to their sacrifice, peace has come to the world.

The suffering of the survivors, too, has value. It will not be easy to live with the Potsdam Declaration. It will not be easy to construct a new Japan on the ruins of the old Japan they loved. But we will get inspiration, says Nagai, from the example of one who sweated blood and carried His cross to Calvary. As His cross had value, ours has value too. And so his story of the bomb is one of triumph. It is a story of resurrection in the very moment of crucifixion. It is a story of chiming bells that announce good news as they peal across the atomic waste.

In all this it is clear that Nagai speaks as a Nagasaki Christian. His little hut is close to that hill on which the twenty-six martyrs were crucified. Martyrdom was a glorious act of which the Nagasaki

Christians are justly proud. And those who died in the atomic holocaust are no less martyrs than their illustrious ancestors who were crucified on mountains or who died hanging over the sulfur pits of Unzen.

In the postwar years Nagai became a symbol of strength and optimism, a central figure in the spiritual and moral reconstruction of Japan. He was partly responsible for the deeply rooted idea that the Japanese, the first and only people to have suffered an atomic holocaust, have a vocation and a mission to abolish war, especially nuclear war, from the face of the earth.

His greatness did not go unrecognized. Before he died he received a visit from no less a personage than Emperor Hirohito; and his funeral in April 1951 was a great event in the history of the city. And today when Nagasaki is still a place of pilgrimage—a place of pilgrimage for those who honor the martyrs, a place of pilgrimage for those who march from Tokyo and Hiroshima, a place of pilgrimage for people of all nations who pray for peace in the Peace Memorial Park—in this place, too, Nagai has his modest little shrine, the tiny hut where he prayed for peace as he lay dying.

Nagai, a great spiritual leader of Asia, has a message for the world. For the fact is that we are now in the quandary foreseen by the scientists who wrote the *Franck Report* in 1945. The arms race has escalated. As I write these words, fifteen thousand physicists from forty-three countries are appealing to the United Nations and to individual governments to halt the arms race. They cite the danger of a holocaust that could kill one hundred million people; they state that some fifty thousand nuclear weapons are currently deployed with a combined destructive power of one million times that of the bomb that wiped out Hiroshima. At the same time, ecologists are saying that a billion people could die before the mushroom cloud (how many times bigger than the one so graphically described by Nagai!) even dissipates.

And as scientists protest I am reminded of Einstein's letter found unopened on Roosevelt's desk. I am reminded of Churchill's comment that everyone at Potsdam took it for granted that the bomb would be used. Is there an answer?

Earlier, I said that Truman was so conditioned by the spirit of the times, so carried along by the collective unconscious, that he could make no other decision than the one he made. In a sense, he had to drop the bomb. Today, however, world leaders are in a more complex situation than Truman. The spirit of our times is less clear: our collective unconscious is divided within itself. On the one hand, there is a longing for peace in the hearts of millions, expressing itself in a powerful movement that demands the abolition of nuclear weapons. On the other hand, powerful inner forces are impelling world leaders to carry on an arms race they cannot halt. The problem is not that some people love peace and others do not. The problem is not that some nations want peace and others do not. The problem is that in all of us, as in all our countries, there rages a struggle between our love of life and our love of death, between our love of self and our hatred of self, between our love of construction and our love of destruction, between our love of peace and our love of money and power. In short, a titanic struggle is raging in the collective unconscious of humanity.

Nagai, in the last chapter of his book, says that, in his opinion, the answer to our predicament is authentic religion. And that raises the question whether authentic religion can revolutionize the collective unconscious and bring about world peace.

Let me pause here to make the observation that there is authentic and unauthentic religion. During the Second World War there was plenty of religion around, just as there was plenty of religion in the Crusades and other holy wars. But was that religion authentic? I would like at this point to relate one significant religious fact.

Before the *Enola Gay* set out for Hiroshima with its murderous "Little Boy" and before *Bock's Car* set out for Nagasaki with its cruel "Fat Man," the military chaplain prayed over the crews. Listen to his prayer:

Almighty God, Father of grace, we pray you, let your grace come down upon the men who will fly in this night. Guard and protect those of us who will venture forth into the darkness of your heaven. Lead them on your wings. Guard their bodies and their souls and bring them back to us. Give us all courage and strength for the hours that lie before us, and reward us according to the hardships they will bring. But above all, my Father, give your world peace. Let us go our way trusting in you and secure in the knowledge that you are near to us now and for all eternity. Amen.

What a diplomatic prayer! Who could quarrel with it? Neither Christian nor Jew nor Moslem could find fault. Yet one wonders if it is good to be ·diplomatic toward God who sees the heart— toward God who loves the thousands who will be blown to smithereens. When religion is manipulated by impious communists or by pious capitalists it becomes very, very unauthentic.

Authentic religion, be it Christian or Jewish or Moslem or Hindu or Buddhist, is based on conversion of mind and heart, on profound enlightenment, on revolution in consciousness. It transforms the whole person; it transforms the unconscious; and when a significant number of people are converted it transforms the collective unconscious. In the modern world this transformation will only be authentic if it brings us to love our neighbor and to a radical commitment to world peace.

Nagai stands before us as a model of such religious conversion. His influence on the collective unconscious of Japan was very great. His impact on the modern world could also be great. It is true that his message is not sweet and easy. His life reminds us that revolution in consciousness only comes through prayer and suffering. But this need not make us discouraged. Throughout our modern world thousands of people are willing to suffer, to go to prison, and even to die for the cause of peace. Millions are praying for peace. A profound revolution in world consciousness is taking place before our eyes. And herein lies our hope for the future.

Let me conclude my introduction by quoting Nagai's poignant cry:

Men and women of the world, never again plan war! With this atomic bomb, war can only mean suicide for the human race. From this atomic waste the people of Nagasaki confront the world and cry out: No more war! Let us follow the commandment of love and work together. The people of Nagasaki prostrate themselves before God and pray: Grant that Nagasaki may be the last atomic wilderness in the history of the world.

Sophia University, Tokyo.
December 8, 1983

NOTES

1. Truman, Harry S. *Memoirs, Volume 1: Year of Decisions*. New York: Doubleday, 1955, 415.
2. Toland, John. *The Rising Sun*. New York: Random House, 1970, 867.
3. Second Vatican Council (1963–65), "Gaudium et Spes," Chapter 5, No. 80.
4. Truman, *Memoirs*, 419.
5. The text of the *Franck Report* can be found in *Hiroshima: The Decision to Use the A-Bomb*. Edited by Edwin Fogelman. New York: Scribner's, 1964, 59–62.
6. *Time Magazine*, February 23, 1948.
7. Churchill, Winston. *The Second World War, Volume 6: Triumph and Tragedy*. London: Cassell, 1954, 553.
8. Toland, *The Rising Sun*, 890.

1
Just Before

It was August 9, 1945. As usual, the sun rose quietly from behind
Mount Kompira; and beautiful Urakami welcomed its last morning. Along the river, the chimneys of the munitions factories belched
white smoke. The tiled roofs of the shopping district next to the
main road looked like purple waves. From the residential district on
the hill rose the smoke that told of happy families gathered together
for breakfast. The terraced fields on the mountain slope sparkled
as the dew glistened on the sweet potatoes. In Asia's number one
cathedral, crowds of Christians, wearing white veils, prayed and
made reparation for the sins of the world.

In the University of Nagasaki, lectures began punctually at 8
A.M. "Fight and study!" was the slogan of the National Volunteer
Army. And every class, every research institute, every hospital
building was organized into a relief corps, each with its own specific
duty. Professors and students wearing air-raid dress and with first-
aid kits at their sides devoted themselves to lectures, to study, to
treatment of the sick. In case of an emergency everyone was at
his or her post to give help to air-raid victims. Air raids we had
experienced many times already. In particular, in the previous week
the university had been bombed and three students died instantly
while more than ten were seriously wounded. But, thanks to the
courageous action of the students and nurses, not a single patient
was hurt. The university was already accustomed to war.

The air-raid warning screamed out. From the lecture halls, students poured into the corridors, formed themselves into groups, and dispersed to their respective positions. The people in charge ran quickly through the corridors shouting orders through megaphones. Today, as usual, there must be a large-scale raid on southern Kyushu. Again the air-raid warning sounded. Looking up at the clear morning sky, my eyes were caught by a flashing cloud high, high up. Enemy planes were approaching. How eerie was the sound coming from some invisible place up there. One after another, from here and there, the sirens wailed and screamed. "I can hear! I understand! Your meaning is all too clear!" But the sirens continued to scream and to be silent, to scream and to be silent, until I felt like covering my ears to shut the whole thing out. What kind of courage did this wailing give us?

The crape myrtle flowers were deep red. Deep red also were the oleanders. The canna were red, red like blood. The first-year medical students who were appointed to be stretcher-bearers stood alert at the shelter near the hospital entrance enjoying the shade of the red bushes and waiting for any emergency that might occur.

"How is the war really going?" asked a young student from the middle school of Kagoshima. "Many of my classmates are going for military training. What's really happening?"

"What are our planes doing?" asked a voice with an Osaka accent from within the shelter. "It's awful! What's the use of fighting? What chance do we have?"

No one answered. Everyone was dimly aware that this voice from Osaka was talking sense. But wasn't Japan, our fatherland, locked in a life-and-death struggle? Our leaders had begun this war with the intention of winning it. They had not raised the curtain on this tragedy just to be defeated. And yet, after the fall of Saipan the language of the General Headquarters smelled strange: it was somehow suspect. The more sensitive students quickly saw this. It was quite obvious they were ill at ease.

"Fujimoto! What do you think? What's going to happen in this war?" The fellow with the Osaka accent showed his red face from the narrow entrance of the shelter. He was wearing horn-rimmed glasses and looked a bit like an octopus peering out of its hiding place.

Fujimoto, the class president, had been standing motionless beneath a phoenix tree with his arms folded, looking intently at the sky. He was a small man with iron nerves. From his steel helmet to his tightly bound black puttees his uniform was perfect and his manners impeccable. Many times he had rescued the wounded from the danger of the bombs, thus winning the confidence and approval of his comrades. When they saw this little man plunge into the smoke and fire, they followed him without hesitation. He always carried the binoculars he had received from his father. He would take them out when enemy planes appeared overhead and, scanning the sky, give a report on their movements.

"What's going to happen in this war?" persisted the boy from Osaka.

"What about the war?" said Fujimoto, as though suppressing his real feelings. "Our fate won't be determined by the war: the fate of the war will be determined by us. What counts is the strength and perseverance of young Japanese or young Americans. According to that, victory will fall to one side or the other."

"But the situation is too bad. The difference in material resources is tremendous. Our little efforts are just useless."

"That may be true. But listen. If bombs start falling on the town below, what's the use of all your theorizing and speculation? Get going and stop the flow of blood! I'm going to do my duty to the end." Fujimoto spoke with decision and resolution. But the boy from Osaka remained unconvinced.

Just at that moment, the vice-president of the class appeared carrying a huge piece of timber. He was a graduate of Kokura Middle School, a man who did his job with few words. His only concern now was to strengthen the observation post. Working alone, he was bathed in perspiration.

"Hey," said a voice addressing the vice-president. "If the enemy really invades, what are we going to do?"

"There's a time to live and a time to die," said the fellow from Kokura as he opened his fan and cooled his perspiring face. "Whether we live or die, we don't want to be the laughingstock of the world."

Again a deep silence reigned. The crape myrtle flowers, the oleanders, the canna, red and motionless, looked like congealed blood. The pulsating cries of the cicadas in the camphor trees of the Sanno Shrine flowed through the air.

It was my turn to see to the air-raid equipment. Entering the hospital from the front, I walked along the wide corridor, inspecting everything, until I came to the back door. At the entrance to each ward, students and nurses, dressed in uniform, stood ready for action.

The buckets were filled with water. The hoses were stretched out on the ground. Picks, fire hooks, shovels, spades—everything was ready for the fight against incendiary bombs or whatever might come. The patients were quietly being carried to the shelter.

In front of the radiology room I ran into a third-year student called Ueno. What a courageous fellow he was! A few days before, when the Department of Gynecology had gone up in flames, he stood alone on the roof of the neighboring dermatology building supervising everything. As we ran to the burning buildings to throw buckets of water on the flames, the enemy dive-bombers swooped down, but Ueno stood in the middle of the bombs giving directions and shouting in turn: "Hey! The enemy planes have gone! Everything is O.K. Come out! The fire is still burning!" or, "They're back! Bombs are falling! Shelter! Danger!"

"Courage," I said as I greeted him. And Ueno shyly scratched his head.

"The other day my mom scolded me," he said. "She told me

not to do things just to attract people's attention. 'You're no longer a kid,' she said.''

The people who worked the hand pumps were stationed at the back gate. Everything was well prepared to cope with incendiary bombs and ordinary bombs. Satisfied, I made my way to the east side of the hospital. In the departments of surgery, gynecology, and nose-and-throat, the havoc wrought by the recent bombs was even worse than the wounds inflicted on people's bodies. Here also the oleanders were blooming bright red like blood, while the smell of carbolic acid floated through the air.

A spasm of fear passed through my body.

The all clear rang, dispelling doubts and fears. When I got back to the classrooms, the students were noisily loosening the straps of their steel helmets. Nurse Inoue, who was in charge of information, tilted her head to one side. Her eyes sparkled even more than usual as she made the announcement, ''No more enemy planes over Kyushu.'' She was simply repeating what had come across on the radio. Perspiration lightly covered her red cheeks over which fell three locks of hair.

''Back to class!'' came the cry from headquarters, and the people in charge again ran through the corridors shouting out the message. The students returned to their respective classrooms. The university once again became an ivory tower inhabited by scholars and students in search of truth. At the hospital clinic, patients jostled toward the reception desk, while students, dressed now in white coats, mingled with them preparing to make preliminary tests. On the other side of the corridor from my room was the Department of Medicine. From within I could hear the pleasant voice of the president, Professor Tsuno. Lectures had begun.

2
The Bomb

Chimoto-san was cutting grass on Mount Kawabira. From where he worked he could see Urakami three kilometers down to the southwest. The hot summer sun was shining lazily over the beautiful town and its hills. Suddenly Chimoto-san heard the familiar, still faint sound of a plane. Sickle in hand, he straightened his body and looked up at the sky. It was more or less clear, but just above his head there floated a big cloud the shape of a human hand. Yes, the sound of the plane came from above that cloud. And as he watched, out it came. "It's a B-29." From the tip of the middle finger of the hand-shaped cloud, a small, flashing silver plane appeared. It must have been eight thousand meters up in the sky. "Oh! It's dropped something. A long, narrow, black object. A bomb! A bomb!" Chimoto-san threw himself to the ground. Five seconds. Ten seconds. Twenty seconds. One minute. As he held his breath, an eternity seemed to pass.

Suddenly there was a blinding flash of light; an awful brightness but no noise. Nervously Chimoto-san raised his head. "A bomb! It's at Urakami." And in the area above the church he saw an enormous column of white smoke float upward, swelling rapidly as it rose. But what struck terror into his heart was the huge blast of air like a hurricane that rushed toward him. It came from under the white smoke and rolled over the hills and fields with terrifying speed and power. Houses and trees and everything else collapsed

August 9, 1945. 11:02 A.M.

7

before it. They fell to the ground; they were smashed to pieces; the debris was blown this way and that. Clumps of trees disappeared before his very eyes as this violent force rushed up the slopes of Mount Kawabira. What was it? He could only think of an enormous, invisible bulldozer moving forward and leveling everything in its path. I'm going to be crushed to powder, he thought. Joining his hands in supplication he called out: "My God! My God!" and again he pressed his face to the ground.

Then a deafening noise struck his ears and he was thrown into the air and hurled five meters against a brick wall. Finally he opened his eyes and looked around. The trees were torn from their roots. There were no branches, no leaves, no grass. Everything had vanished. All that remained was the smell of resin.

Furue-san was returning by bicycle from Michi-no-o to Urakami. Just as he was riding past the munitions factories, he seemed to hear the sound of a plane. He looked up and somewhere in the clear sky above Matsuyama, about the height of Mount Inasa, he saw a ball of red fire. It was all red like strontium burning in a huge lantern, but it was not so bright as to blind the eyes. Down, down it came toward the earth. What is this? he thought. And just as he put one hand above his glasses to shield his eyes and see more clearly, there was a sudden blinding flash of light like the explosion of magnesium, and he was hurled into the air. Many hours later he regained consciousness and found himself lying in a rice field, pinned under his bicycle. He realized that he was totally blind in one eye.

At Ogakura School, seven kilometers from Urakami, a teacher, Tagawa, was writing an account of the morning's alert in his air-raid journal. He looked up and his eyes rested on the scene outside the window. In front of him was the foot of the mountain and above was the blue sky of Nagasaki harbor. Suddenly, the sky was illuminated by a flash of blinding light. The noonday sun in the height of summer would have seemed terribly dark compared with what he saw. This light was certainly many times brighter than the sun.

"Are they using flares during the daytime?" Tagawa murmured to himself, and he leaned forward to see what was happening. He saw a strange and marvelous spectacle. "Look! Look!" he shouted. And all the teachers in the room rushed to the window.

In the sky above the Urakami district of Nagasaki, something like a piece of white cloud moving sideways and upward with tremendous power began to swell . . . and swell . . . and swell. "What is it? What is it?" they shouted wildly as it formed itself into a huge mushroom a kilometer in diameter. And then came the rushing blast of wind. The faculty room was shaken to its foundations. The teachers were thrown to the ground and buried beneath an avalanche of broken glass.

"A bomb! A direct hit on the school! Shelter!" Tagawa shouted at the top of his voice as he struggled to his feet and groped his way to the shelter dug into the hill behind the school. And as Tagawa sat all alone on the cold ground, he did not know what God alone knew—that at that moment, at his home in Urakami, his wife and children, calling his name, drew their last breath.

South of Nagasaki harbor on the hillside of Mount Hachiro about eight kilometers from Urakami is the village of Oyama. From here one can see the basin where Urakami lies, and beyond one can see Nagasaki hazily in the distance. Young Kato was taking his cow to pasture. In the expanse of green, he found some wild strawberries and he was picking them and putting them in his mouth.

And then came the flash. The cow saw it too and lifted her head. In the sky above Urakami rose a white cloud—a deep white cloud like an enormous ball of cotton—and it got bigger and bigger and bigger. It looked like a huge lantern wrapped in cotton. The outside was white but inside a red fire seemed to be blazing and something like beautiful electric lights flashed incessantly. The colors within this lantern were now red, now yellow, and now purple—all kinds of beautiful colors.

Next, the cloud took the shape of a bun. And then, as it gradually went up and up, it began to look like a mushroom. From the part of Urakami that was directly below the white mushrooming cloud, black smoke and dirt seemed to be sucked into the air—and this too went up and up. The mushroom-shaped cloud above rose higher and higher into the clear sky. When it reached a great height, it collapsed and began to flow toward the east. As for the dirt and smoke below, it rose higher than the mountain. Then part of it began to fall down and disperse, while another part flowed with the cloud to the east. Since the weather was clear, the light of the sun lit up the mountain and the sea. Only Urakami, directly below the cloud, fell under a great shadow and looked completely black.

And then came the blast! Kato's clothes were torn to shreds. The leaves of the trees were blown away. And yet the blast of wind had already weakened considerably when it reached him. The cow did not run wild. Kato supposed that another bomb had fallen nearby.

Takami-san was returning to Koba with his cow. He was walking along the Odorise road, about two kilometers from Urakami, when the flash took place. He felt heat, as when one warms oneself at a brazier, and both he and his cow were burned. Then, all of a sudden, balls of fire rained down on them with a swishing sound. One such ball struck his foot. White smoke shot up and the flames fizzled out leaving a smell like the one that remains when a paraffin lamp has been extinguished. Fires broke out all around.

3

Immediately After

The university buildings were between three and seven hundred meters from the center of the explosion, so they were within the radius directly affected by the bomb. The classroom of fundamental medicine was close to the explosion and, since it was a wooden structure, it was immediately smashed to pieces and burned. All the professors and students died instantly. The classroom of clinical medicine was somewhat further away and was made of concrete, so fortunately there were some survivors.

It was shortly after 11 A.M. I was in my room on the second floor above the dispensary for outpatients. I was choosing X-ray films to teach the students the art of diagnosis. And before my eyes the flash of blinding light took place. It was like a thunderbolt in a clear sky.

A bomb must have fallen at the very entrance to the university, I thought. I immediately tried to throw myself to the ground, but before I could do so, the glass of the windows smashed in and a frightening blast of wind swept me off my feet into the air—my eyes wide open. Pieces of broken glass came in like leaves blown off a tree in a whirlwind. I felt that the end had come. The right side of my body was cut and gashed by the glass and warm blood flowed down my cheek and around my neck. I must have a large wound above my right eye and around my ear, I reflected. But I felt no pain.

It was as though a huge, invisible fist had gone wild and smashed everything in the room. The bed, the chairs, the bookcases, my steel helmet, my shoes, my clothes were thrown into the air, hurled around the room with a wild, clattering noise, and all piled on top of me as I lay helpless on the floor. Then the blast of dusty, dirty wind rushed in and filled my nostrils so that I could scarcely breathe. I kept my eyes open, looking always at the window. And as I looked, everything outside grew dark. There was a noise like the sound of a stormy sea, and the air everywhere swirled round and round. My clothes, the zinc roof, pieces of wood, and all kinds of other objects were performing a macabre dance in that dark sky. Then it gradually became cold, as at the end of autumn, and a strange and silent emptiness ensued. Clearly this was no ordinary event.

I again came to the conclusion that a bomb of at least one ton had fallen at the entrance to the hospital. There would probably be about a hundred wounded. Where could we send them? What could we do with them? We must get the teachers together. But probably half of them were dead or wounded.

But I must first get myself out of this wreckage in which I was trapped. I moved my knees and with difficulty stretched out my body. As I did so, everything became black. Were both my eyes completely blind? What a mess I was in! At first I thought that since I had wounds around my eyes there must be a cerebral hemorrhage there. But when I tried to move my eyes I succeeded in doing so. I was not blind.

And, strange to say, when I reached the conclusion that I was not blind I was, for the first time, struck with horror. The buildings had collapsed and I was buried alive! What a weird and grotesque death I was destined to meet. Anyhow, let me do what I can, I thought. And underneath the pieces of debris I continued to struggle with all my might. But I was flattened like a rice cracker lying in a toaster. I couldn't imagine what part of my body I could move or in what direction. I even had to be careful about moving my face since I was lying in a sea of broken glass. Moreover, as it was pitch dark, I didn't know what kind of objects were around me or how they were held in place. When I moved my right shoulder slightly, something fell. "Help! Help!" I shouted. But my voice sounded pitiful as it rang out in the silent darkness.

Nurse Hashimoto was next door in the X-ray room. Fortunately, when the bomb exploded she was standing between a bookshelf and the wall. And so she survived without a scratch. While all the objects in the building were flying through the air as if given life by some mysterious power, she stood glued to the wall counting the seconds. Ten. Twenty. Thirty. All around her whirled dust and smoke that almost choked her, but she stood resolutely waiting. At last the large objects seemed to settle down on the floor once again. Nurse Hashimoto decided that the time had come for relief work, so she climbed out from behind the fallen bookshelves. And what a spectacle met her eyes!

Everything was a shambles. Making her way across the debris, she looked out the window. And then the shock was even greater. What on earth had happened? From this window one had been able to see the purple wave of tiled roofs in the districts of Sakamoto, Iwakawa, and Yamaguchi. But they had disappeared. Where had they gone? And what about the factories that used to belch white smoke? Mount Inasa, which had been buried beneath a luxuriant carpet of green, was now changed into a mountain of bare, red rock. And all that summer green—the green leaves on the trees and the green grass—had vanished, so that not one leaf, not one blade of grass remained. The universe had become naked!

And what had happened to all those people who were crowding the front entrance? As she looked down on the open square, Hashimoto was shocked to see naked bodies lying everywhere among the big and small trees that had been torn up by their roots. Spontaneously she covered her eyes with her hands. "Hell! This is hell!" No one even groaned. It really was the world of the dead.

As she pressed her hands against her eyes, everything went completely dark. She opened her eyes and looked around. There was not the slightest noise. And there was no streak of light in that pitch darkness. She began to think that she was the only person left alive in the whole world, and she was overcome with fear and trembling. She could see the god of death soon sinking its claws into her; and before her eyes floated an image of her home. Her mother's face appeared. Hashimoto raised her voice and began to weep. She was only a child of seventeen.

But then she heard a voice cry, "Help! Help!" It seemed close, yet it must have come from a distance and through several walls. "Help! Help!" came the voice again.

It's the voice of the dean! Dr. Nagai is alive! If he's alive, we can do something to take care of that mass of bodies in front of the building. Hashimoto immediately changed from a sniveling girl to a determined and courageous nurse. Guided by the voice, she tried to go into the next room but got tangled in the electric wires of the X-ray camera so that she could scarcely move her legs. Finally she groped her way to the corner where there was usually a shovel, but it had been blown away, and in its place she found only a megaphone. Remembering that there was a hoe in the X-ray screening room downstairs and that the chief nurse also should be there, and realizing that she must get everyone's cooperation, she left the X-ray room.

Hashimoto was accustomed to walking the dark corridors in the evening blackouts. But now it was different. She had gone only two or three steps when she bumped against something soft. Stooping down and touching it, she realized it was a human body. Her hand rubbed against something wet and sticky like blood. Finding the arm, she then moved down to the wrist. There was no pulse. Sadly she joined her hands in a brief prayer and moved on. Again, after a couple of steps, she bumped against a fallen corpse. As she bent down, wet hair stuck to her hands. It was still pitch black all around. She wondered how many people lay dead in the darkness around her. As she felt for a pulse in the body, she opened her eyes wide and tried to look about her, even though she could see nothing.

Quite suddenly everything became red. Outside the window a fire had broken out. The flames were getting bigger and bigger. What a horrible sight lay before her now that she could see by this red light! Almost unconsciously she dropped the wrist she was holding and stood up. The red light flooded down the broad corridor of the hospital to reveal the convulsed bodies of the dead. Some were on their knees. Some seemed to be grasping the empty air. Some seemed to be struggling to their feet. And thus they had died.

Hashimoto knew that she could do nothing alone. First she must get together a rescue team: this had to be the work of an organized group. She must assemble the people at the place where the dean lay buried beneath the debris. "Forgive me! Forgive me!" she said to the dead as she stepped over their bodies. And she made her way down to the examining room.

The people in the X-ray screening room were in the process of putting together the apparatus for examining X-rays. Suddenly they heard the sound of a plane.

"What's that?" exclaimed Nurse Tsubakiyama.

"It's a B-29," said technician Shiro, and he kept manipulating his forceps.

"They've dropped a bomb!" cried technician Choro, who had been injured in the thigh during the raid a few days before. "Let's get to a safe place. Shelter! Shelter!"

All three dived under a large table. And then came the flash.

"Another bomb has fallen!" screamed Shiro. But his voice was drowned by the blast of wind that swept through the room. They remained still, waiting for the storm to subside. Tsubakiyama held her breath. Finally she asked, "Is anyone hurt?"

"No. What about you?"

"I don't feel pain anywhere."

"Hey! Chief Nurse!" cried a loud voice.

"Yes," came the familiar, charming voice from the neighboring room. "A lot of stuff has fallen on top of me."

At that moment there was a terrible roar all around. Everything became pitch dark, as when a train enters a tunnel. While they looked at one another, the pale face of Nurse Tsubakiyama disappeared from sight.

"What on earth is this?" It was Choro's voice.

"It's a new kind of bomb like the one that fell on Hiroshima." This was Shiro.

"No. The sun must have exploded," said Choro.

"Maybe so . . . the temperature has suddenly dropped." Shiro's voice was thoughtful.

"If the sun explodes, what happens to the earth?" Now it was the anxious voice of Nurse Tsubakiyama.

"It's the end of the world," said Choro with resignation.

They remained silent and waited. No light returned. A minute passed. Someone's watch kept ticking in the darkness. Tick, tick, tick. . . .

"What about lunch?" It was Shiro's voice.

"I already had mine. Did you bring yours?"

Choro sounded as though he wanted a final meal before dying. "All right," he said. "Let's divide the lunch and eat before we die."

And then, just as when a train emerges from a tunnel, the surroundings gradually lightened. Choro's white teeth. Shiro's long nose. Tsubakiyama's charming little dimple.

"Ah, the sun was all right after all," said Shiro.

"But share that lunch!" urged Choro. And the three crawled out from beneath the narrow table over the powdered glass, the fragmented machinery, the smashed chairs, the tangled electric wires.

"Where on earth did the bomb fall? Only a direct hit on this room could cause this kind of damage. But I don't see a hole in the ceiling."

The atomic cloud, as seen from a street in downtown Nagasaki five minutes after the blast.

"Did you hear the noise of the bomb falling?"

"No, I didn't hear a thing."

"I wonder if it was a kind of altitude bomb."

"Anyhow, it was a diabolical thing."

Chief Nurse Hisamatsu bounced in from the next room like a

rubber ball. She was stroking her tangled hair with both hands as she asked: "Is everybody O.K.?"

Just then a first-year student nurse popped out from somewhere and, throwing her arms around the chief nurse, began to cry.

"Don't be silly!" said the chief nurse. "You're alive, aren't you?" But the young student kept on crying. A friend had died right before her eyes.

"Well, put on your helmets and look for the bandages," said Nurse Hisamatsu; and with calm self-control she went to a place where water was running from a pipe, quietly washed both hands, washed her face, washed her mouth, and gargled with water. "I feel as if I'd taken a deep breath of gas," she said, and, as though she wanted to rinse out her lungs, she washed her mouth again and gargled four or five times.

"Tsubakiyama, come and wash your hands. If you handle gauze with those grubby hands, the wounds will only get infected. Tomokiyo, you too, come and wash your hands and face. Fuse, get ready at once. There are an awful lot of wounded people around." The chief nurse kept wiping her hands as she gave orders.

"All right," replied Tomokiyo and Shiro. "O.K." said Choro and Fuse. And immediately they complied with the orders.

And then there was a crackling sound. Tsubakiyama ran to the window. "A fire! A fire!" she cried. And all five, picking up buckets that were lying there, rushed to the water tank. In the open space in front of the old, unused X-ray room, a heap of timber that had not been cleared away when everything else was evacuated had caught fire; there was a sea of small flames. Following the instructions they had received in training, they began to throw buckets of water on the fire, concentrating their efforts on one spot. But alas, the fire was not confined to one place. The corridor of the hospital was now engulfed, and the dining room was collapsing as it sent forth flames everywhere. All that remained was the concrete wards. The wooden buildings had vanished and in their place was a lake of fire. All five kept throwing water on the flames, but they were spreading rapidly and getting out of control. It became obvious that these buckets of water were of no avail.

"Let's save the machines," said Shiro.

"Let's help the wounded," said Choro.

"Let's take the patients to a safe place," said Tsubakiyama.

As they watched, the flames were spewing black smoke; and they realized that an enormous fire was going to develop.

"Let's get orders from the dean," said Nurse Hisamatsu.

And at that moment Hashimoto appeared. "The dean! Dr. Nagai! He's buried alive!" she cried.

They looked at one another. "He's so big! How will we be able to get him out?" blurted out little Tsubakiyama.

"It's O.K. We'll manage," said Choro as he rushed to the door.

Following Hashimoto's lead, all five jumped over the wood and over the fallen desks, giving one another a helping hand as they made for the X-ray room. The usual route was blocked and they could not pass. So climbing out the window and grasping a pipe, they climbed around, anxious above all to save their dean. But the window of the pharmacy room was high up, and in order to get there they had to form a human ladder. Choro grasped a gas meter and became the base; Shiro got on top of him. Then the chief nurse and Tsubakiyama climbed over them and got in through the window. Then Shiro climbed in. And finally they all pulled up Choro by the hands—hands that looked like the claws of a lobster. "Wow!" he shouted in his characteristic way. And in he jumped.

In the developing room, Professor Fuse was just about to remove an X-ray picture from the developing tank. Suddenly he heard the student stationed at the observation post on the hill behind the hospital shout out: "Enemy plane entering air space directly above. Shelter! Shelter!" And in the next moment he heard the familiar sound of a plane high up in the sky. Thinking it was a dive-bomber, he was going to throw himself to the ground; but, reflecting that his pictures might be destroyed, he washed them and placed them gently in the fixing tank. And then, as he was about to crouch down, the blow fell and he was knocked unconscious.

When he regained consciousness, he was lying on the floor with some pieces of wood on his chest pinning him to the ground. Somehow he succeeded in moving and in freeing his waist and hands, and bit by bit he was able to remove the wood piled on top of him. He looked around to see what had happened to the photographs in the fixing tank, but his glasses had been knocked off and he could not see clearly.

But what had happened to Moriuchi-san who had been working beside him? Again and again he called out to her, but there was no answer. He searched underneath all the fallen wood, but there was no sign of her. She must have got out in the nick of time, he supposed.

Crossing over the heap of rubble and going into the corridor, he was completely stunned. It was as though he had come to an utterly unknown place for the first time. The whole scene was entirely changed. Was it because he had lost his glasses? Two or three times he rubbed his eyes and looked around.

Until now I have related the stories of people who had the good fortune to be in concrete buildings and were not directly exposed to the radioactive rays. But what about the people who were out in the open?

Behind the Department of Pharmacy, Professor Seiki and his students were hard at work digging a shelter. The professor was digging inside, while the students were carrying the earth away. Who could have guessed that at that moment they were drawing lots? Those outside were choosing death, while those inside were choosing life. Wearing short pants, they looked like miners as they vigorously dug into the ground. They were some four hundred meters from the center of the explosion.

A blinding flash lit up the dugout to its very depth. Then came the terrible roar. Tomita, who, basket in hand, was working at the entrance, was blown inside, hitting the back of Professor Seiki who was crouching down and working with his spade.

"What's going on?" shouted the professor angrily, as he straightened his back. But after Tomita, pieces of wood and shreds of clothing and bits of tile came hurtling through the air. A big piece of wood hit the professor full in the back and he fell unconscious in the mud.

Only a few minutes seemed to pass. Professor Seiki regained consciousness and found himself lying in a maelstrom of smoke and fumes filling the shelter. The hot air kept pouring in, but the professor, tottering to his feet, made his way to the entrance. At first he felt relieved that he had survived. But the feeling of relief did not last long. Unconsciously he dropped his spade and stood aghast with mouth and eyes wide open, dazed by what he saw.

The large buildings of the Department of Pharmacy were no longer there. The biochemistry classroom was not there. The pharmacology classroom was not there. The fence was not there. The houses outside the fence were not there. Everything had disappeared and all that remained was a sea of fire.

Atomic specialist and doctor of physics though he was, Seiki did not realize that this was an atomic bomb. He never dreamed that American scientists had made such progress.

But what about the students? He looked at the ground around him and a cold shiver went through his whole body. "Is it possible that these lifeless beings are my students? No, it can't be! In the shelter I was struck in the back and I'm still unconscious. It's a nightmare. No matter how awful war is, it can't be this cruel." He pinched his thigh. He felt his pulse. Yes, his body was awake and alive. "If this isn't a nightmare, what is it? It's worse than any dream."

The professor went quickly to the first charred body that lay nearby. "Hey! Hey!" he shouted. But there was no answer. He grabbed the shoulders with both hands and tried to lift the body, but the flesh peeled off like the skin of a peach. Okamoto was dead.

The boy beside him groaned and turned over. "Murayama! Murayama! Hold on!" cried the professor as he cradled in his arms the student whose skin was peeling off. "Professor! Professor! . . . Ah!" And with these words Murayama rolled over on his side. He was dead. With a deep sigh, Dr. Seiki laid the cold, naked body on the earth, joined his hands in silent prayer, and crouched down beside the next charred body.

Araki was swollen like a pumpkin and the skin was peeling off his face. But the narrow white eyes were open as he said quietly, "Professor, I'm finished. There's no hope for me. Thanks for everything."

Blood flowed from the ears and noses of the dead and dying students. Some had had their skulls smashed and had died instantly. Evidently they had been thrown violently to the ground. There were others from whose mouths bubbles of blood were flowing like froth.

Tomita, the only other person not critically injured, went quickly among them giving them water to drink and uttering words of encouragement. Not a single one of them could move by himself. After helping one and moving on, Tomita would look back only to find that the moaning student had become silent. He was dead.

In this way twenty students, one after another, breathed their last. But two men alone could not help all these people. Would no one come to their assistance? Professor Seiki shouted out: "Help! Help! Someone come!" He faced north and shouted. He faced east and shouted. Then he faced west and shouted again. He strained his ears and listened. But the atmosphere had not yet returned to normal. Restless gusts of wind were swirling fiercely on all sides. And mingled with the sound of that wind, from beneath the broken and crushed roof, he could hear endless cries, voices screaming for help.

"Help! Help! I'm in agony!"

"Come, somebody!"

"I'm burning! Throw water on me! Water!"

"Mommy! Mommy!"

The professor felt dizzy. Again he lost consciousness and fell to the ground. After some time he opened his eyes to find that a thick, black, solid cloud filled the whole sky. The sun had lost its light and looked like a reddish brown disc. It was dark like evening. It was cold.

Seiki strained his ears and listened. The number of voices crying for help had somewhat diminished. The child screaming for its mother must have been burned to death.

The first-year students were quietly taking notes. Their ears were not yet accustomed to the sound of the Latin words used in the anatomy class. But they were beginning to feel like full-fledged doctors as they followed the words of the professor and proudly wrote horizontally in roman script.

Then the sudden flash. Total collapse of everything. The professor had not even time to pause in his sentence. The students had not even time to raise their heads and look around. Just as they were, sitting attentively in the classroom, they were crushed beneath the heavy roof.

Fujimoto, the class president, found himself caught under a beam or something, but it was not extremely heavy. All around was pitch dark. He began to choke as he breathed the dust and smoke that swirled about. But eventually he managed to free the trunk of his body and to move into the narrow space between the benches. Beside him people were groaning. Others were shouting out. But counting the voices he realized that few of his eight companions were still alive.

And now through the cracks in the timber the smell of burning began to filter in. Soon hot, stinging smoke was flowing in. A fire had broken out; and, in a moment of panic, he realized that he must work fast if he was to survive. He tried to free himself and to get up, but the beams, the planks, the tiles, and the earth piled above him were too heavy and he could not move them. The crackling sound of the flames came closer and closer. I might be burned to death any minute, he thought. And he pushed. He shoved. He gathered all the strength of his head and shoulders and back and of his whole body, but he was unable to move the weight a single inch. He thought of the laws of mechanics, but it was useless to make such calculations here. The wind blowing through the cracks in the debris gradually became hotter, and the reflection of the red flames dancing this way and that became more brilliant.

Suddenly someone began to sing "Umiyukaba": "If I go to the sea . . ." It was a strong, full voice and it continued to sing slowly. Fujimoto lost all his strength. Now he lay back without resistance, straining his ears to listen to the last, glorious, patriotic song of his friend. "I shall not return . . . ," sang the voice. And the song came to an end. "Good-bye, my friends," said the voice. "I am slowly burning to death from my feet upward."

After a couple of minutes I, too, will burn to death, reflected Fujimoto. He knew his fate. He joined his hands in silent prayer and saw the face of his father. "Be calm," his father seemed to say. Then he saw his mother's face. The form of his young brother, Masao, floated before his eyes. Yes, Masao would become a doctor in his place. One by one he recalled the faces of his companions in the X-ray room. Until he entered the university and received his student cap, he had worked as a technician in this department. What had happened, he wondered, to his close friend Tako-chan—the "Little Octopus"—who took the exam and entered with him? The few words that he exchanged with his radiology companions each morning and evening—these also floated through his mind.

"Don't panic," said Fujimoto to himself. "Why panic when you're a prisoner, trapped in this narrow strip of debris with no way out, when you're about to be burned to death, reduced to cinders and ash? Your body, it's true, has no defenses, no power to act. But soon your soul will launch across the universe undisturbed, imperturbable, and serene. There's only a minute of imprisonment left.''

The smell of burning flesh struck his nostrils: the sweet smell of young bodies burning. ''My body will smell sweet too,'' he reflected. ''This is the greatest moment in my life and yet the most ordinary, too. Yes, it's that simple. In the end, what is the body? It's just for assimilation and rejection. Just for eating and digesting, for urination and defecation.'' In spite of himself, Fujimoto gave a wry laugh.

But now he recalled the words Professor Fuse often addressed to students working for examinations: ''When you cannot solve a problem, think of the contrary.'' Yes, that's it! In a moment of illumination, instead of looking at the debris above he began with his hands to feel the floor beneath. His fingers found a split between the boards. With all his power concentrated in those fingers, he began to pull a board upward. He could do it. With a crack the board yielded. When the atomic blast had struck the ground, it had rebounded up on the boards, loosening the nails. He pushed his hand down under the board and drew it up. How delicious was the sound as the floorboard separated and the air of salvation rushed in! A second and a third board came away quite easily. And suddenly Fujimoto fell through the floor to safety on the ground beneath.

Dr. Yamada and Tsujita-san had just returned from the station where they had bought their tickets for Tokyo. They opened the back window of the classroom in the bacteriology department to let in some fresh air so that they could relax. The two women were about to go to the Institute of Contagious Diseases in Tokyo where they would take a course in serum treatment. Eventually Nagasaki's hour of seige would come: they must quickly prepare in this area as in others. Most of the men had gone to the field of battle, so the burden of responsibility rested on the shoulders of these two young women scientists.

Weeds were growing in the tennis court. Sports and recreation were things of the past, forgotten some years ago when the war effort took priority over everything else. Beyond the tennis court stood the tall camphor trees and pine trees, and further on was the playing field, now turned into a rich sweet-potato field. And over all towered the big, red cathedral.

Two girls, wearing wide pants, waved as they crossed the tennis court. It was Hama-san and Oyanagi-san, nurses in the X-ray department. Tsujita-san had formerly worked as a technician in this department, and seeing her face at the window they greeted her warmly. Tsujita-san, in turn, stood up and waved her hankie.

In the sweet potato field, the former playing field, Yamashita, Yoshida, and Inoue, nurses in the same department, were crouching pulling weeds. Here and there on the terraced fields of the slopes of Urakami, farmers, taking advantage of the end of the air-raid warning, could be seen doing the same work of weeding. A long line of worshipers was making its way to the cathedral, their umbrellas shining brightly as they walked.

"How beautiful Nagasaki is! One never tires of looking at it."

"Yes. But when we return from Tokyo two months from now, will it be like this?"

"Something tells me that Nagasaki is going to be destroyed."

"Something tells me that Nagasaki alone will survive."

And then the flash.

Dr. Yamada threw herself on the floor and thus was saved. She alone survived to tell the tale. Beside her, Tsujita-san fell dying. "Oh! the pain! The pain!" she gasped. And with these words she died. It was like a dream. The bacteriology classroom became a ball of fire. Professor Naito and all the others were killed instantly.

When Dr. Yamada dragged herself out of the building, everything was dark and the wind was moaning. And what a scene met her eyes! The huge pines and camphor trees were torn up by the roots and all the school buildings had collapsed. As for the cathedral, about one-third of the building was blown down, in-

Urakami Valley—the atomic wilderness. In the center is the cathedral.

cluding the fifty-meter-tall bell tower, and the remnant looked like a ruin of ancient Rome. On the stone fences, people were hanging upside down with arms and legs torn off. The road was dotted with fallen men, women, and children. In the fields, innumerable corpses lay as far as the eye could see. Dr. Yamada thought about the nurses who had waved from the playing field. What had happened to them? No doubt they had been blown asunder and lay motionless on the ground. Everybody outside seemed to be dead.

Dr. Yamada herself had not sustained any serious wound. Nevertheless she felt something abnormal in her whole body. Scarcely had she taken four or five steps when her knees gave way and she lay down hopelessly on a sheet of zinc that was on the ground. Beside her lay an old German textbook on bacteriology. This kind of learning is useless now, she reflected. And she used the book as a pillow.

And there she lay. Her mind wandered off into an agonized world of pain and anguish as she waited desperately for help in her distress.

4
Relief

On August 9, 1945, at two minutes past eleven in the morning, a plutonium atomic bomb exploded at an altitude of some five hundred meters over Matsuyama in the center of the Urakami district of Nagasaki. Tremendous energy was released. And this energy, a tempestuous blast of air traveling at a rate of two thousand meters per second, smashed, pulverized, and blew apart anything in its path. The void created at the center of the explosion sucked up everything on the ground, carrying it high into the sky, and hurled it back violently against the earth. The heat of 9000° Fahrenheit burned the surrounding area. Fragments of incandescent metal rained down in balls of fire immediately setting everything alight.

It is estimated that thirty thousand people lost their lives and that more than one hundred thousand received light or serious wounds, while countless others were afflicted with atomic diseases caused by radiation. In some cases the symptoms of these diseases appeared immediately; in others they appeared much later.

The cloud of smoke in the sky, caused by the bomb and the debris that had been sucked up, hid the rays of the sun, bringing a total darkness like an eclipse. After about three minutes, however, as this immense cloud of smoke and dirt grew bigger, it scattered and became less dense. And once again light and heat filtered down to the earth.

As I have already said, I myself was buried beneath a heap of debris. But finally I managed to extricate myself by my own efforts and make my way to the photography room where I found Professor Fuse with Nurse Hashimoto, the chief nurse, and the others. They all ran to me. "Oh, good! Good!" they kept shouting as they threw their arms around me joyfully.

I looked at their faces one by one. How precious life is, I reflected. How good that you are alive!

"But people are missing," I said. "What about Yamashita? What about Inoue? What about Umezu? Let's look for the others and help them. Come back here in five minutes." And with that we left the room and scattered in all directions.

Professor Fuse and Shiro went to the developing room. Pulling away pieces of rubble and looking underneath, they kept shouting: "Hey! Hey!" and strained their ears. But there was no answer. "Moriguchi, are you alive?" roared Shiro. But all was silent.

Choro brought back Umezu seriously wounded. He had found him amidst the instruments in the radiotherapy room. Covered with blood, Umezu threw himself down in the corridor. "I've lost my eyes," he whimpered.

"Don't talk nonsense! Your eyes are all right," said Choro, examining the wound. Above his eyes was a deep gash and there were cuts all over his body.

"It's all right, it's all right," said the chief nurse encouragingly as she applied iodine, put some gauze on the wound, and skillfully bandaged it.

I took Umezu's pulse and gave some instructions about how we should treat the wounded.

"Doctor, help me!"
"Give me medicine!"
"Look at this wound!"
"Doctor, I'm cold. Give me clothes!"

A strange group of naked human beings crowded around us, all shouting. These were the people who somehow survived when everybody and everything was swept into the air and hurled in all directions by the explosion.

Since the bomb had fallen just when the outpatients were coming in great numbers for consultation, this part of the corridor and the waiting room were littered with an enormous number of fallen people. Their clothes had been torn off; their skin was cut and peeling away. Covered with dirt and smoke, they were gray like phantoms, and it was difficult to believe they were human or that they belonged to this world.

Some, in whom a spark of life remained, extricated themselves from the vast and motionless heap of dead flesh and crawled up to me. Clinging to my feet, they cried: "Doctor, help me! Doctor, help me!" Someone held up a wrist from which blood was pouring profusely. "Mommy! Mommy!" screamed a little girl as she ran this way and that. And mothers, writhing in agony, kept calling the names of their children. "Where's the exit?" roared a big man as he ran around. "Stretcher! Stretcher!" shouted agitated students. And the whole place fell into deeper and deeper turmoil and confusion.

We began emergency treatment. But we quickly ran out of bandages and had to tear shirts, using the strips to bind the wounds.

No sooner had we treated ten or twenty victims than from behind came more and more shouting, "Help me! Help me!" On and on they came and it seemed there was no limit to their number. Since I had to keep one hand pressed tightly against my own wounded forehead, I found it difficult to work. Whenever I removed this hand in order to attend to a patient's wound, the blood would spurt out like red ink from a water pistol, splattering the wall and the shoulder of the chief nurse. An artery in my temple had been cut. But since it was a small artery, I thought my body would hold out for about three hours. Sometimes I felt my own pulse and then went on treating the patients.

Hashimoto and Tsubakiyama, who had gone in search of their friends, came back. And their report was grim. "They're nowhere to be found," they said. "They probably went to the playing field. We tried to get there but the way was blocked by fire and fallen trees and dead bodies. The fundamental medicine buildings are gone. Everything is a mass of flames. The center of the hospital is one big fire and there's no way of reaching the back entrance. The number of wounded is just incalculable." Such was their report.

Yamashita, Inoue, Hama, Oyanagi, Yoshida—the faces of these five nurses floated through my mind one by one. Were they dead? Or dying? Were they seriously wounded and writhing in agony like the patients before my eyes? Or were they safely sheltering in some quiet place? Yet, if they were alive, they would certainly have come here to join us. Anyhow, something ghastly had happened, something that does not ordinarily take place in the course of war. This was a cruel tragedy of unprecedented dimensions. Undoubtedly it would be counted among the significant and terrible events in human history. Yet it was a situation we must confront with quiet determination.

I returned to the X-ray room and sat cross-legged on the ground. Dr. Fuse and the chief nurse put medicine on my wound, and, pressing some gauze tightly against it, they tried to stop the bleeding. Over the gauze they put a triangle of linen and again pressed tightly. But it was an arterial hemorrhage. The bandage quickly became bright red and the blood, flowing down my cheek, began to drip from my chin.

"Everyone check the instruments," I said. And they all quickly disappeared, dispersing to various rooms.

I did some serious thinking. The place had become a bloody field of battle. We were the ambulance corps. Our real work was just beginning; we must stand with determination. Doubtless the enemy would continue to drop these bombs. Within a week he would invade our shores and fighting would break out. This was no time for wavering. If we fell into confusion, we would be able to do nothing. We must assemble the core staff members and get organized.

We must make sure we had sufficient supplies of medicine and food. We must prepare a camp. After that, we had to establish an efficient system of communications and choose a suitable place in the country for a hospital. Sooner or later Nagasaki would be bombarded from the sea. We must get the patients quickly away and reassemble in a nearby valley.

I looked out the window. I could see nothing but a forest of fire. The whole neighborhood had become one great mass of flames. The fire had even spread to one corner of the building in which we were, and now we could hear the crackling of the approaching flames.

Those who had gone to examine the instruments came back one by one. "The whole thing is a mess." "The valves are all destroyed." "The electric wires are cut." "We couldn't drag out the transformer because the way was blocked." "The specimens have been blown away and we can't find them." All the reports were harsh and cruel.

The eyes of all were fixed on me and everyone waited for me to speak. Professors and students and nurses from other departments, in twos and threes holding hands and covered with blood, passed by hastily without saying a word. We could hear the roar and crackle of the flames, and sparks began to blow in through the window. What was I to do?

I looked at the faces around me. It was important not to panic. Yet, if we just kept calm doing nothing, we would burn to death. We couldn't remain inactive. As these thoughts passed through my mind, I broke out in a nervous laugh. So sudden and unexpected was my reaction that everyone joined me in a burst of laughter.

"Look at the state you're in!" I said. "You can't go to war like that. Get ready! Get prepared! And we'll meet in front of the main entrance. Don't forget your lunch! You can't fight on an empty stomach."

"Let's go!" they shouted enthusiastically and returned to their rooms. As I watched them depart, I realized that they were all back to normal.

Dr. Fuse got my shoes, and the chief nurse found my steel helmet and my coat. And slowly I made my way to the main entrance. In the corridor in front of the Department of Gynecology, a nurse with a wild look walked round and round and round. I slapped her vigorously on the back. "Come on. Be brave!" I said. But she didn't seem to notice and kept walking round in circles. The shock had been too much for her and had made her temporarily insane.

The space in front of the main entrance was littered with dead and wounded. Moreover, from downtown mutilated people kept coming and coming. Holding their wounds, they asked for the first-aid station and for the hospital reception. In addition to this, groups of people carrying the wounded on their backs or on their shoulders stumbled out of the hospital wards, pressing round me at the entrance. What on earth was I to do?

Each life was precious. For all of these people the body was a precious treasure. All were preoccupied with their wounds, big or small. They wanted to be treated by a competent doctor. This was the situation I must somehow face. But then, with this multitude of wounded, with our fast-vanishing medicine, with the flames pressing in, with so few of us . . . after treating just a few of the wounded I knew that if I did not take a comprehensive view of this situation we would all be engulfed in the flames with the very victims we were bandaging and trying to save.

Already twenty minutes had elapsed since the explosion, and Urakami had become a flaming landscape. From the center of the hospital, flames were spreading through the whole campus. The only place free from fire was the hill on the east side of the hospital. Pumps, hoses, water tanks, energetic people—anything or anyone capable of quenching those flames had vanished in a moment. Only one possibility remained: to allow the flames to spread and spread.

Even the survivors were penetrated by powerful radioactive rays. Their clothes were torn and many of them were completely naked. From downtown they ran, climbing the mountain with tottering steps in an effort to escape the flames. Two children passed by dragging their father. A young woman ran clutching a headless child. An aged couple, hand in hand, slowly climbed the mountain. As she ran, a girl's clothes burst into flames and she fell writhing in a ball of fire. On top of a roof that was enveloped in flames, I saw a man dancing and singing wildly: he was out of his mind. Some people kept looking back, looking back as they ran; others did not even turn their heads. A girl was scolding her little sister who lagged behind, but the little one begged her to wait. And from behind the flames pressed on.

About one in ten people had had the good fortune to survive. The others lay charred and dead beneath the wreckage of their burned houses.

As the fire roared on, the direction of the wind changed and from far and near it carried the sound of voices incessantly crying for help. I stood aghast, with folded arms, contemplating the spectacle. Never in my life had I felt so deeply my own impotence. Was there no way of helping these suffering people who were rushing to death before my very eyes?

"Doctor, you look like the fiery temple guardian!"

I looked around. Two third-year students, Nagai and Tsutsumi, were standing beside me. My students of the X-ray department had also come together, all prepared for action. And Moriuchi, who had plunged into a dugout, showed up safely. Then someone came running up and threw her arms around the chief nurse. It was Kosasa-san, the X-ray technician in the gynecology department. She had saved two nurses from the heart of the fire and rushed here frantically through the flames. Now the only ones missing were Sakita-san and Kaneko-san, X-ray technicians in the dermatology and surgical departments.

I made my decision. "The machines can wait. Let's attend to the people," I said.

Dividing into groups of two, they carried the wounded from the burning wards. Kosasa and Moriuchi went back into the raging fire in search of Sakita and Kaneko. Choro took Umezu on his back and made his way up the mountain. The whole scene was like a picture from the Russo-Japanese War.

As we reentered the building, people who had finally succeeded in extricating themselves from the rubble under which they had been buried came running out, fleeing for their lives with wild and flashing eyes. Panic-stricken, they did not know what they were doing. But if they leave the hospital, I thought, where will they go and who will take care of them? "Don't panic!" I shouted. But they paid no attention to my cry.

I went to the operating room in the basement, only to find that a pipe had burst and the whole place was flooded with water. I then made my way to the next room where the medicines and instruments were stored, but here the scene was even more heartrending. Even the stretchers were smashed and thrown here and there, while the surgical instruments were scattered all over the floor. The containers of liquid medicine, powdered medicine, and fluid for injections were smashed and thrown into one great mess on top of which water kept flowing from a pipe.

Ah! Was it not for today that we assembled all this material? Was it not for today that we practiced with those stretchers and gave all those lectures on relief work? And now we were confronted with total failure. Like a mosquito whose legs have been plucked off, like a crab whose claws have been torn away, we faced a multitude of wounded people, helpless and empty-handed. It was really primitive medicine that we were now reduced to. Our knowledge, our love, our hands—we had only these with which to save the people. Crestfallen and depressed, I climbed the steps and, standing in the entrance, surveyed the whole situation once more.

Discouraged though I was, I knew that around me stood doctors and nurses and students—about twenty people in all—who would work till they dropped. The groups of two who had gone from room to room to pick up the wounded now returned and put them in the coal shed beside the entrance. This was the only place that was safe from falling sparks.

I stood helplessly in the middle of them, doing nothing. The fire was becoming more and more violent. Black smoke swirled round and round in the sky; and the thick cloud, reflecting the color of the fire, glowed with an ominous red light. It was an utterly disheartening scene.

"We've saved the president!" cried a voice. It was Tomokiyo standing in the doorway holding a bright red mass of something. Running to him, I saw that the red heap was none other than the president, Professor Tsuno. From his white hair and his face to his white coat and trousers and socks, he was totally soaked in blood. His glasses were gone.

"Ah! Nagai. It's terrible. But you've done well," he said.

I felt his pulse. It was not particularly weak or irregular. "The hill at the back is safe," I said to Tomokiyo. "Take him two hundred meters up that hill and find a suitable place where he can rest."

Professor Fuse prepared an injection and followed them up the hill. The president had been attending to the outpatients when he was struck down. Dr. O had also incurred a serious wound. He had helped the president out into the corridor but collapsed from loss of blood and was unable to stand up. It was just then that Tomokiyo came upon them and was able to help them.

Maeda-san, chief nurse in the internal medicine department, now rushed from the ward and, seeing me, asked: "What about the president?"

"He's O.K.," I replied. "Dr. Fuse is with him up the hill at the back."

Her face was deadly pale and blood was pouring from above

her eyebrow. Yet she immediately rushed toward the hill. I watched her as she disappeared from sight. How could such a plump nurse climb that rocky hill with such agility?

But let me say a word about two of our own nurses.

Hashimoto was seventeen years old and Tsubakiyama was sixteen. For both of them, their height in proportion to their girth was a bit unusual. We liked calling them by their nicknames: "Little Barrel" and "Little Bean."

Short and stocky Little Barrel and Little Bean made their way into the waiting room where seven patients and students were writhing in agony on the ground. They found a big fellow lying at the entrance and together they gently put their arms around him, lifted him up, and carried him down the steps to the coal shed. Then they immediately returned and picked up the next person in the same way. And so they took care of three or four people; and when they had finished their work in that room, they moved to the consultation room beside it.

Here they found a nurse with whom they were vaguely acquainted. Taking her in her arms and carrying her downstairs, Little Barrel was filled with a deep joy such as she had never experienced before. It was a noble joy accompanied by profound happiness. "This Nurse Hamazaki, who's moaning faintly, doesn't know that I'm carrying her out of the flames in my arms. If Little Bean doesn't tell her, she'll never know that we saved her life. If we come through all this alive, we'll meet her in the corridor and she'll give a little bow and pass on without any idea of what's happened." And as she reflected on this, a smile vibrated through her cheeks.

She associated it with the pure joy she had experienced in childhood. As a child she had kept red berries in an empty cream bottle and preserved them with salt. She kept this bottle hidden in a corner of the little storeroom in a place that she alone knew. Her sister knew nothing about it and her brother had never been able to find it. Morning and evening she would secretly go to this place and eat one berry. She would gaze at these beautiful berries as if they were rubies or some other precious stone.

Meanwhile, Little Bean was entertaining quite different thoughts. Why are these adults so light? In the past she had carried wounded and sick people to the ambulance. In the consultation room she had helped lift patients from the trolley to the X-ray bed. And even when three nurses carried them, the people seemed really heavy. But now they were light. This was strange. Probably their weight had diminished from loss of blood.

She thought of Professor Nagai's air-raid training. It was too tough. If actual war was only as fearful, as painful, and as difficult as what she was now experiencing, then the training need not have been as fearful, painful, and difficult as Professor Nagai had made it. Soon after entering the nurses' training college she had undergone a test of courage. The technicians, senior students, and nurses, imitating the dead and wounded, were lying groaning in a dimly lit room. Then the first-year students, who had not yet studied anatomy, had to go into this room and feel the pulse of the so-called wounded and dying. It occurred to her that the fear that had come over her then did not arise today, when she was holding in her arms real dead and wounded people.

Again, she recalled the exercises for carrying people, and how they had tied ropes around their bodies on the steep and dizzy mountainside of Arakobo. That was much more frightening than the reality she now faced. Or there was the practice in putting out fires. A real incendiary bomb was thrown into the room, and she was told: "Extinguish this at once or it will become a real fire!"

And then she began to think about her friends Koyanagi-san and Yoshida-san with whom she had spent the last year. Together they had cried and laughed. Together they had undergone training and worked during actual air raids. She felt lonely without them. But they were separated from her by the flames and she did not know whether they were alive or dead. And yet she somehow felt they would come back. Little Bean put her head out the window and shouted: "Yoshida-saaan! Yoshida-saaan!"

Little Barrel, standing beside her, put her head out too and shouted: "Inoue-saaan! Mitsu-chaaan!"

But there was no answer. The flames continued to roar and the buildings were collapsing nearer and nearer the very place where they were standing.

When they went to help the next patient, they saw that the fire had spread and the number of rooms engulfed in flames was increasing. And yet, as they crawled into those rooms enveloped in fire with hand towels tightly bound around their noses and mouths and dragged out the wounded, they experienced a thrill of joy such as they had never known. Coming out of the awful heat, they noticed that their cuffs were on fire. Yet they both felt the ecstatic joy of being nurses.

It was easier to handle the patients who were unconscious. Those who were conscious kept giving trouble, complaining that their wounds were hurting or they had some other pain, so please carry them slowly. Or they asked us to go back for things they had forgotten; or they wanted tissue paper. In this way, without realizing it, they wasted precious time. Moreover, they did not know the awful tragedy that had befallen Nagasaki with this bomb, nor did they understand the extent to which the flames were enveloping the hospital. And so they infuriated us with their little demands.

In the internal medicine ward was a patient with acute rheumatism of the joints. Dr. Okura and Yamada took him in their arms and tried to leave the room. But he screamed out in agony, crying that rather than endure such pain he preferred to remain where he was. So they had no option but to take out the other patients. At last, since he was the only one remaining, they turned again to him. Once more they put their arms around him. But he complained that he wouldn't go unless they brought a stretcher. So they searched everywhere but were unable to find one that was serviceable. By that point they had wasted a lot of time; and when they returned to the room, they found it engulfed in flames.

"There's only one left. He refuses to come!" cried Dr. Okura, running to me with anguish in his voice.

"You've done all you can," I said. "I take responsibility for that patient."

But the faces of the two men were full of pain. They seemed to feel responsible for the man's death as they stood looking up at the ward in which tongues of fire were already flickering and dancing.

I looked at my watch. It was two o'clock. Before we realized it, three hours had passed. The fire was now at its height. For quite some time the wind had been blowing from the west. Flames, tens of meters high, rose up into the sky as far as the eye could see. They seemed to be vying with one another to see which could go highest until, pressed by the wind, they collapsed toward the east.

Since the wind was blowing toward the university, the coal shed began to be in danger, and I decided that the patients must be taken to the field further up the hill. But what a task that proved to be! The path was narrow and blocked with the wreckage of houses, and we had to climb over bare rocks and stone fences carrying the patients one by one. I myself climbed up twice, each time taking a patient on my back. But when it came to a third, I knew that my strength had left me and I could not go on. My temple artery had not stopped bleeding and I had had to change the bandage three times. The chief nurse warned me that my face was ghastly pale and I realized that my pulse was very weak.

Little Barrel and Little Bean deftly lifted a big man on their shoulders.

A baby howled and howled. The mother, seriously wounded, lay unconscious. And beside her lay this baby, about two months old with a protruding navel, crying wildly. Since the fire was approaching rapidly, I felt that I must at least save the baby. So I took her in my arms and, climbing up the hill, laid her close to Nurse Hamazaki. Just at that moment Hamazaki uttered a deep groan and slumped over on her side. Sensing that her end had come, I took scissors and cut a lock from the front of her hair and put it in my pocket. Yamada and the chief nurse, saying that it was too terrible to separate the baby from her mother, took the woman in their arms and carried her up. When they laid the baby at her mother's breast, she howled all the more. The hand of the unconscious mother moved toward her child.

Large drops of rain began to fall. It was black rain, the size of the tip of one's finger. When it splashed on something, it left a stain like that made by crude oil or some such thing. It seemed to come from the dark cloud above us.

And now the situation was becoming even more ghastly. The oxygen in the air had been used up by the fire, and there was an extraordinary upsurge of carbon dioxide, so that it was difficult to breathe in this valley of flames. As we worked, we were panting like dogs.

When I next looked at my watch, it was four o'clock. The patients had been brought safely up the hill and were lying in the field. The students, acting as scouts, were running here and there searching for some kind of roof to cover them. But there was fire everywhere and there was no better place than this for the wounded and dying.

We sat down and had something to eat. The nurses at first protested that they were too emotionally keyed-up for food; but when I explained that this situation might well continue for days or even months, they all sat down for this strange meal.

When we had eaten, we calmed down and were able to relax. Now we could listen to the complaints of the patients one by one and we began to give them careful and loving treatment. We fixed the bandages, tied up the wounds once more, replaced the triangular gauze, applied iodine and gave them water to drink. We found quilts and drapes to cover them. We applied splints.

"Smoke is pouring out of the specimen room!" It was the voice of young Nagai.

Ah! Those specimens, the fruit of more than ten years of sweat and toil! The irreplaceable and precious photographs! All these were turned into a cloud of smoke.

"The photography room is burning! It's good-bye to our medical instruments!"

Giving all our time to the care of the patients, we had been unable to save the specimens and the instruments. The documents and records that had been our daily food, the specimens that were tokens of our scholarly progress, all those instruments that we had loved like our own hands, our own children—were now changed into red flames shooting up into the heavens. Before our very eyes, countless memories were being turned into black smoke and were vanishing from sight.

We stood silent and stupefied, staring at the awful scene. The fire became even more violent. It entered the cellar where our films were stored and belching out black smoke and red flames it exploded with a deafening roar. My knees trembled and I felt all my strength ebbing away. "It's the end," I murmured and collapsed in the field where I stood. The chief nurse and the others around her broke out weeping and sobbing.

The university had become one big ball of fire. It was indeed the end. The president, Professor Tsuno, had suffered serious wounds. No one had seen the director of the hospital, Professor Naito, and it was presumed that he had met the same fate as the hospital itself. According to the students' reports, only Professors Koyano and Cho were safe. Almost all the others had vanished, though someone reported that Professors Kitamura and Hasegawa had been rescued by hospital workers and had been seen covered with blood climbing the hill at the back. Eighty per cent of the students and nurses had died. Among those who survived, many were seriously wounded. Combining my group, consisting mainly of people from the surgery department, and another group from the dermatology and pediatrics departments working at the rear entrance area, the total number of survivors was about fifty.

Since we despaired of any survivors from the rooms of fundamental medicine, we had to admit that in terms of personnel and equipment the university was utterly destroyed. We who were standing on the hill looking at the last traces of that burning university, we were the heroic soldiers of the era of Showa.

From one of the hospital rooms, Dr. Okura brought out a big white sheet. Taking a handful of the blood that was dripping from my chin, I traced a huge circular sun on the sheet, which now became a Japanese flag. Attaching this "Rising Sun" to a bamboo pole, we lifted it up and watched it flutter loudly as the hot wind blew all around.

With sleeves rolled up and a white band around his head, young Nagai grasped the pole with both hands and raised the flag high in the air. And then he moved slowly forward carrying the bloody Rising Sun up that hill covered with black smoke. And we all followed in solemn and silent procession. It was five o'clock in the afternoon.

Thus our Nagasaki School of Medicine lost the battle and was reduced to ashes.

5

That Night

Together we made our way to the field where the university president was lying. Seeing him in a corner of the sweet potato field, all curled up, covered with an overcoat and soaked by the rain, I could not restrain my tears. Under the direction of Professor Cho, students were running here and there giving help to the wounded. I made a report to the president about what had happened and began to walk away.

No sooner had I taken twenty or so steps than I felt dizzy and realized that my legs were giving way under me. Nevertheless, seeing Umezu lying on the ground, drenched by rain but under the watchful care of Choro, I bent down and took his pulse. It was unusually strong and I felt greatly relieved. Taking off my coat, I put it over him and rose to go on. But hardly had I taken five or six steps down one of the terraces when I felt my head swimming. And finally I collapsed unconscious on the ground.

"Press the carotid artery." I recognized the voice of Professor Fuse. "Put pressure on the nape of the neck."

I opened my eyes and looked up to see the anxious faces of Professor Fuse, the chief nurse, Little Bean, and technician Kaneko looking down at me.

"Thread! . . . Forceps! . . . Gauze! . . . Gauze!" The doctor was shouting excitedly as he thrust something into the wound around my ear, causing me acute pain. I heard a cold, metallic sound as warm blood spurted out and flowed over my cheek.

"Press down! . . . Wipe it clean! . . . Gauze!" Intermittently I could hear the doctor shouting. Sometimes the tip of the forceps seemed to pinch the very fiber of my nerves. Tremors of pain vibrated through my body and my toes seemed to tighten with pain. Almost unconsciously my hands clutched the grass on which I was lying.

I saw Dr. Cho hasten to my side; Dr. Fuse was saying something to him in a whisper; again someone was feeling my pulse. I closed my eyes, prepared for the worst.

"The end of the artery has fallen behind the bone," said the professor. And again my toes seemed to tighten with pain and my hands kept clutching the grass.

But the operation was eminently successful.

"Dr. Nagai, everything is all right. The bleeding has stopped," said the professor as he straightened up.

I thanked him. And then quite suddenly a heaviness spread through my body and I again lost consciousness.

When I opened my eyes, the whole earth was still blazing fiercely, while the dark cloud that covered the sky was shining uncannily with a red light. Only to the west, above Mount Inasa, a small portion of the sky was visible and the thin, sharp crescent of the moon could be seen.

In the valley above the Konan ward of the hospital, groups of men were picking up planks and gathering straw to make provisional huts, while the women were preparing the evening meal cooking pumpkins in steel helmets. Young Nagai and Tajima went to the prefectural office to get emergency rations. The rest of us made a little circle around the fire where the pumpkins were being cooked.

A little circle of survivors. As we looked at one another we felt that we, the men and women who formed this small group, were bound together by some incomprehensible fate. Grasping one another's hands and holding tightly, we sat there in silence.

From the darkness of the wood above came pitiful cries:

"Stretcher! . . . Get me a stretcher!"

"Won't someone give me an injection?"

A voice crying for a friend. A voice crying for a father or a mother. A familiar voice. The great cry of a number of voices raised in unison.

We sat very still. We were resigned to the death of seven of our companions. Nurse Sakita of the dermatology department was lying in a ditch seriously wounded in the leg and unable to move. Fujimoto had had a narrow escape when he fell through the floor of the auditorium. A short while before he had passed close to us leaning on a stick and we told him to go home.

But what about Kataoka (affectionately called "Little Octopus") and Tsujita and Yamashita and the other nurses, five in all? If a spark of life remained in their bodies, they would have returned to our department. That was the kind of people they were. So deep was our relationship that even if they were mortally wounded and their souls were about to leave their bodies and were bound to them only by the hair of their heads—still they would make their way here to breathe their last at our side. But eight hours had passed with no sign of them and we could only presume that they were dead. We bowed our heads in silent prayer.

A big, naked man clumsily made an appearance. "Dr. Nagai!" he cried. "At last I've found you!"

"Dr. Seiki! You're alive!"

"I'm the only one," he replied as he sat down heavily on the ground.

The blackened piece of timber he had been using as a stick fell from his hand with a dull sound. His shoulders heaving and breathing heavily, he looked like a huge, wounded bull.

"Come at once," he panted. "The students are dying. More than half of them are already dead. Come and give them injections. We can't leave them to die like this. They're in a shelter at the pharmaceutical school."

"We'll go immediately. But wait a moment . . . have some pumpkin."

"I've no time for pumpkins. A hundred pumpkins won't save these students. Let's go at once."

Dr. Fuse, the chief nurse, Hashimoto, and Kosasa grabbed their first-aid kits and stood up. Dr. Seiki, receiving a helping hand from Shiro, finally got to his feet.

"The university is finished," he said. "It's awful. Everyone is dead. The way here was just appalling. It took me an hour to come three hundred meters. But I must go back. Good! Now we'll be able to help the students."

Leaning on the shoulder of the chief nurse, the doctor staggered back into the burning university.

And so we divided into groups.

One group spent the night helping the wounded on the hill behind the classroom of fundamental medicine. Dr. Okura and Nurse Yamada and the others continued their treatment from the hut, which was now completed. Umezu and I were ordered to sleep on the straw inside the hut. And what a night it was! Death and desolation were all around us. Even the insects had been exterminated.

Meanwhile the rescuers, relying on the light of that huge fire which scorched the earth and filled the sky, and guided by the anguished cries that arose everywhere, made their way to the wounded and dying. They bound their wounds, gave them injections, took them in their arms and brought them to the shelter on the hill. Sometimes the road was blocked unexpectedly by a curtain of flames and they changed direction, only to find a barrier of fallen trees that they could not pass. At other times they climbed over stone walls that had collapsed in the blast. Or again, not seeing that a wooden bridge had been blown away, they fell into a ditch together with the patient they were carrying. Nails had pierced the soles of their shoes, and their bleeding feet gave them excruciating pain with every step. Their knees, cut by broken glass and covered with blood, stuck to their trousers.

They found Professor Takagi, head of the medical department, and succeeded in bringing him to safety. Next they came back carrying Professors Ishizaki and Matsuo. And as more and more people were brought in, the hut was filled with moans and cries. The daughter of Dr. Tani, head of the pharmaceutical department, was seriously wounded. An insurance company employee came and made his way in. And two prisoners begged for help.

Twice enemy planes flew overhead and with a dull sound dropped bundles of leaflets.

Toward midnight the fire at last began to die down. Whether they were dead, or resigned to their fate, or fell asleep from fatigue—whatever the reason, the cries of the wounded ceased completely. And a great silence reigned on the earth and in the sky. It was a solemn moment in Nagasaki.

And it was a solemn moment in Tokyo, too. For just at this time, in the Imperial Palace, His Majesty the Emperor was making the decision to bring the war to an end.

The Second World War, a drama that had been played on every continent and every ocean of the globe, this great war which had gradually spread beyond human control until no one knew what endless suffering it might bring—this war had suddenly reached a climax with the appearance on the stage of a new actor: the atomic bomb. Now, quite unexpectedly and quite suddenly, the curtain was falling on this terrible drama. Surely it was a solemn moment.

With overflowing heart I stood contemplating the sky over which the ominous radioactive cloud hovered. In which direction was this atomic cloud floating? Toward good or toward evil? Toward justice or toward wickedness?

One thing was certain. At that moment and in that sky, the curtain was rising on a new age: the atomic age.

6

The Power of the Bomb

On August 10 the sun as usual showed its gentle face; but its light was welcomed not by a beautiful Urakami but by an Urakami of ash. Not by a living city but by a city of death.

The factories were lying in ruins. The chimneys were broken. The shopping district was a mass of shattered tiles. In the residential district only the stone steps remained. The fields were stripped naked. The wood was burned to the ground. The tall trees had been violently torn up and strewn about like matches. Desolation reigned everywhere. Not a single dog was left alive to move around in that place of death. In the middle of the night the cathedral had suddenly caught fire sending huge sheets of flame high into the sky, as if to put a final period to that sentence of death.

At dawn we moved to the shelter at the pharmaceutical center and began to help the wounded. In a corner of the playing field someone was lying face down under a sheet of zinc. It was Dr. Yamada of the bacteriology department. From her we learned about the last moments of Nurse Tsujita.

Next we made our way to the Department of Bacteriology. In the ashes of the burned-out laboratory we discovered heaps of charred bones. Were they the bones of the professors who had been working there?

Going to the room that Professor Yamada had indicated, we

49

found the skeleton of a woman. This must have been Nurse Tsujita. What heartache! Never again would these bones laugh that jolly laugh we had come to love. Picking up the bones and putting them in a sheet of paper, I kept thinking to myself: "If only it were a dream! If only it were a dream! . . ."

Next we came to the auditorium where Little Octopus had been attending class. Among the ashes, which shone white in the sunlight, lay a number of skeletons in a row. Was Kataoka-san, our Little Octopus, among them? While the students held their pens to take notes, their young lives were snatched away in the space of a split second. Yesterday morning they had passed merrily through the university gate, proudly wearing their university caps!

And then the awful thing we had feared and expected. Yes, our fears became a tragic reality when we approached the sweet potato field, the former playing field, and found five bodies. We had waited and waited but they had not come. We had called and called but they had not answered. Here they were. Their hands were raised above their heads.

Probably what had happened was that Nurses Hama and Oyanagi had walked over to where Nurses Yamashita, Yoshida, and Inoue were pulling up weeds. They approached from behind and said some words of greeting. The others stood up to speak to them. And then, just as they were saying good-bye and hurrying away, the crash came and they were struck down. All five lay there with upraised hands. The two groups were slightly separated one from the other.

So young and innocent were the victims that the chief nurse could not believe they were dead. Grasping their shoulders, she called them by their familiar names: "Hide-chan! . . . Mitsu-chan!?"

If I had known that these kids would die so soon, I would not have been so hard on them, I reflected as I gazed at Yamashita's pretty little nose. I put my hand on her icy forehead. Yes, I was always scolding little Yamashita but I loved her more than Inoue to whom I never said a hard word. On her breast remained a badge in the shape of a little dog, while loose earth was clinging to her lips.

But the bomb which in one moment had claimed all these lives and caused such unspeakable destruction—what kind of thing could it be?

The chief nurse came running up and handed me a sheet of paper. It was one of the leaflets dropped by enemy planes the previous night. As I glanced at it I shouted out spontaneously: "The atomic bomb!"

In the depth of my being I felt a tremendous shock. The atom bomb has been perfected! Japan is defeated!

Yes, yes, that's it, I thought. Such destructive power can only be the atomic bomb. I considered all that had happened since the previous day, and it tallied in every detail with what we were expecting from the phenomenon of the atomic bomb. Had this laborious work of research reached perfection? The victory of science: the defeat of my country. The triumph of physics: tragedy for Japan. Conflicting emotions churned in my mind and heart as I surveyed the appalling atomic wasteland around me.

A bamboo spear lay on the ground. I kicked it fiercely and it made a dull, hollow sound. Grasping it in my hand, I raised it to the sky, as tears rolled down my cheeks. The bamboo spear against the atomic bomb! What a tragic comedy this was! This was no longer a war. Would we Japanese be forced to stand on our shores and be annihilated without a word of protest?

These are the words that were written on the leaflet:

To the People of Japan

Read carefully what is written in this leaflet. The United States has succeeded in inventing an explosive more powerful than anything that has existed until now. The atomic bomb now invented has a power equal to the bomb capacity of two thousand huge B-29s. You must reflect seriously on this terrible fact. We swear that what we say here is the solemn truth.

We have already begun to use this weapon against the Japanese mainland. If you still have doubts, look at the destruction caused in Hiroshima by one single bomb.

Before this bomb destroys all the military installations that are prolonging this useless war, we hope that you will petition the emperor to stop the war.

The President of the United States has already given you an outline of thirteen conditions for an honorable surrender. We advise you to accept these conditions and to begin rebuilding a new and better peace-loving Japan. You must immediately take measures to bring to an end all armed resistance.

If you do not do this, we are determined to use this bomb and other excellent weapons to bring this war to a swift, irresistible conclusion.

I read the leaflet once and was stunned. I read it a second time and felt they were making fools of us. I read it a third time and was enraged at their impudence. But when I read it a fourth time I changed my mind and began to think it was reasonable. After reading it a fifth time I knew that this was not a propaganda stunt but the sober truth.

With a bamboo spear in one hand and the leaflet in the other, I returned to the air-raid shelter where Professor Seiki was lying.

"Um!" groaned the great professor as he rolled over on the ground. And he remained there silent, gazing at the empty sky, for nearly an hour.

If the atom explodes, what happens? This was the question that filled my mind as I lay beside the naked body of Professor Seiki. And four topics came to my mind for consideration: the enormous power of the atom, the elementary particles, the heat, the electromagnetic waves. Let me say a word about each of these.

First, the enormous power.

By enormous power I mean the force that exists in the atom from the very moment of its creation, especially the force in the atomic nucleus. This is the force which maintains the form of the atom and is the source of its activity. It is tremendous energy compared with the volume of the atom, and it is the motive power behind the changes and movements of everything in the universe. Some scientists even hold that the gigantic quantity of energy emanating constantly, day and night, from the sun is nothing other than atomic energy from the constant explosion of the sun's atoms. If this is true, we could call the atom bomb a man-made, or artificial, sun.

When this enormous atomic force is released, it immediately and simultaneously exerts pressure on everything within a certain radius. The phenomenon, however, probably differs according to whether the explosion takes place in a vacuum, on earth, or in water.

In Nagasaki the explosion took place in the air. The energy emitted pushed the molecules of air in all directions, and a tremendously powerful outward wind pressure spread over the surrounding area. In this way a vacuum was created at the center. And after the great wind pressure came negative pressure.

Since the explosion took place over Urakami which lies in a valley, the spherical blasts of wind collided with the walls of the valley, creating a tumultuous situation. To put it briefly: the principal pressure came first to the ground, pushing down, crushing, breaking in pieces and blowing asunder everything that was there. There then followed the negative pressure which pulled everything in the opposite direction and sucked things up. Light rubble and debris were carried up in the sky forming a black cloud of dust. After that, complex wind pressures mingled with one another and raged for some time. It is not surprising, then, that people found themselves torn this way and that, without knowing where they were being pulled. The velocity of this atomic pressure was more or less the same as that of sound waves.

My next consideration was elementary particles.

The elements that fly about as initial particles are atomic constitutive particles such as neutrons, protons, alpha particles, negative electrons, new atoms created by the fission of the atomic nucleon, and original atoms that did not split.

Among these, the neutron plays the most important role. Since the neutron is a small, electrically neutral particle, when it leaves the atomic nucleus with a certain initial velocity, it travels in a straight line at that velocity without receiving any influence from electric or magnetic fields. It then pierces through objects. Its velocity is probably thirty thousand kilometers per second. However, when it collides with the hydrogen atom, it stops. Thus, it can be stopped by water, moist earth, or paraffin.

As for the alpha particles, the proton is charged with positive electricity and the electron with negative electricity. The initial velocity of the particle as it leaves the nucleus may change when it is influenced by electric and magnetic fields. Positive and negative may join together. Or the particles may get an electric discharge in the air. Perhaps most of these float in the air without reaching the ground.

The new atom produced by the fission of the atomic nucleus is smaller than the original atom. For a certain duration it is unstable and continues its radiation. But its volume being large, the resistance it receives is also large; and gradually losing velocity it floats in the air. Eventually it will come down and lie on the ground as radioactive fallout. Consequently, for some years it will be a source of residual radioactivity, particularly in the area at the center of the explosion away from the wind.

These groups of initial particles diffuse spherically when they explode. After being conditioned by the velocity, gravity, buoyancy, and atmospheric pressure, they take a certain shape. When they are in the center, water vapor may condense. Indeed, the atomic cloud that appeared immediately after the explosion was caused by this condensation of water vapor. Probably the black rain was also produced in this way.

My next topic was heat.

Since enormous changes like this take place in an instant, great heat is naturally generated. All objects close to the center of the explosion were burned. For example, the signpost at the entrance to the pharmaceutical department building still stands with the side facing the center of the explosion burned black. Black objects, which attract heat, were particularly badly burned. Let me give some examples of this.

The iris region of Inoue's eyes was pierced. The surface of black tiles became foamy. Some patients' skin was badly burned only on those parts of the body covered by black clothing. And black parts of stones were most affected.

The remains of a young bomb victim.

My fourth and last topic was the electromagnetic waves.

As a result of the sudden change in position of the electrified particles within the atom, there are distortions in the electric and magnetic fields and these are radiated as electromagnetic waves. If we place them in order, beginning with the shortest wavelength, they are: gamma rays, X-rays, ultraviolet rays, visible light, infrared rays. There may exist electric waves with still longer wavelengths. The velocity of each of them is amazing: 299,790 kilometers per second. The moment they struck the eyes with a flash—that was the moment of the atomic explosion. Instantly, terrible gamma rays pierced human bodies, and infrared rays badly burned the exposed parts.

Choro and his companions had gathered around Dr. Seiki and were engaged in heated discussion.

"Who on earth really perfected this work? Was it Compton? Or was it Lawrence?"

"You can be sure that Einstein played an important role. And then Bohr and Fermi and the other scientists who were exiled from Europe to the United States."

"Then the British scientist Chadwick who discovered the neutron—and the French, the Joliot-Curies."

"We've been cut off from scientific research for years now and the important literature hasn't been published. So I don't really know. But quite certainly new scientists have emerged. And then, knowing the United States, you can be sure that thousands of scientists were mobilized. No doubt they divided up the research and worked with tremendous efficiency."

"But it's not all laboratory work. A great deal of industrial energy is needed just for mining the material, refining, smelting, analyzing, and purifying it. Eventually the whole thing will be made public, and then we'll realize that in comparison with their scale Japan's Arms Research Institute is just a matchbox thrown on the street beside the Maru Building. Probably the energy of several thousand workers went into making one atom bomb. The few hundred Japanese schoolgirls working with paper and paste on our secret weapons are no comparison."

"I wonder what kind of atoms they used? Uranium perhaps?"

"I wonder. Maybe they used a lighter material like aluminum."

"But if they used such tiny atoms, the power released would also be small."

"But uranium crude ore is scarce throughout the world. I wonder if there's any element that one can get easily enough and in sufficient quantity for a war like this."

"Don't worry! Canada produces any amount of uranium."

"Speaking of materials, I wonder how they managed to bring about the atomic explosion just at the right time and with such a large quantity of whatever element they used."

"Well, that's the problem! That was precisely the focal point of competition among physicists the world over. A few minutes ago somebody mentioned the name of Lawrence. He's the leading proponent of the theory of destroying the atomic nucleus by means of a cyclotron."

"How can you put a cyclotron into a bomb? I've seen one in the Research Institute of Physics and Chemistry. It's as large as a big building."

"Perhaps there's some way of making it small."

"No. When you consider high tension insulation or the electromagnet, you can't exactly make it smaller."

"What do you think of using alpha rays or radium or some such thing?"

"Or couldn't they have used the mesotron of the cosmic rays?"

"Ah! I've got it! Yes, that's it! Fission!"

"Yes, yes! Fission! The phenomenon discovered by Madame Meitner."

"Madame Meitner? The name doesn't sound familiar. What nationality is she?"

"She's Austrian. She did her research in Copenhagen. She's also one of the scholars expelled by Hitler. She used to be an assistant to Dr. Hahn. But she must be an old woman by this time, well over sixty. Her research has some connection with the work of Professor Fermi of Italy. She found out that if you make a slow-moving neutron hit a uranium nucleus, the latter breaks in two. A fast-moving neutron is no good because it passes through the nucleus and nothing happens. If the slow-moving neutron creeps into the atomic nucleus and stays there for a while, the nucleus suddenly breaks in two and separates. Then the great atomic energy latent in the nucleus is released and bursts out.''

''Wow! That's brilliant! It can be done with the neutron alone.''

''A very interesting fact is that the mass of the part that was broken in two is less than the original mass. This proves Einstein's theory of the equivalency of energy and mass. That was a revolution in physics—certainly the most important development in the field of science in recent times. In a word, when the nucleus breaks in two, the mass of some of it changes: that's to say, the matter suddenly ceases to exist and the same quantity of energy is generated. The energy of the atomic bomb comes from that.''

''The matter suddenly changes into energy?''

''That's it. When the mass of the matter is multiplied by the square of the velocity of light, the product is the energy of that mass.''

''The velocity of light is about thirty thousand million centimeters per second. So its square comes to an enormous number. I wonder how much energy is produced when one gram of mass is changed into energy.''

''Roughly speaking, when one gram of mass is converted into energy, that energy can carry an object of ten thousand tons for one million kilometers.''

''Wow!''

''As for the bomb that destroyed Urakami, I'm quite sure they used a great number of atoms and several mechanisms. The bomb must have been about the size of a torpedo. But I imagine the mass of the atom actually used was a few grams.''

''That's fantastic! But in order to cause the fission of many atomic nuclei, how do you discharge the neutron?''

''Fortunately, when uranium undergoes fission, it emits gamma rays and usually two neutron particles as well. And these two neutrons, colliding with other nuclei nearby, cause fission in two places. Then another two neutrons come out of these nuclei and cause the fission of four nuclei. Next 8, then 16, 32, 64, 128, 256, 512, 1024, 2048. . . .''

"And so at the beginning there aren't so many but after a short time a tremendous number of atoms explode simultaneously. Which is called a 'chain reaction.' ''

"Then if one neutron first undergoes fission, all the others follow. But strictly speaking it isn't simultaneous. It takes time.''

"That's true. We felt the explosion pressure for more than just a moment. It lasted for a few seconds. I remember that at first it was rather weak and suddenly became strong.''

"What followed after that must have been the pressure coming as a result of the resonance action.''

"Did we know all this in Japan?''

"Yes, we did. Even I know this much.''

"Then why didn't we do it?''

"This experimentation of Meitner's began long before the war. At that time many countries began to experiment. Uranium is the element that causes fission: isotope uranium—U-235 and U-238. U-235 is the best. If there's some other element mixed with the uranium it doesn't undergo fission when the neutron reaches it and, as a consequence, the chain reaction terminates. So, in order to complete the reaction, we have to have a certain amount of pure uranium 235. This is very difficult. In Japan, we'd begun to purify uranium 235, but we were stopped by the military government. They said the army couldn't be allowed to spend so much money on research that was little more than a dream. So we had to give up. At any rate, that's what I've heard.''

"What a pity!''

"No use regretting what's past. It is really unfortunate when wise people have ignorant leaders. But let me tell you one more thing. I said that after the fission of the nucleus, the neutron comes out. However, if the lump of uranium is very small, the neutron jumps out into the air and again the chain reaction terminates."

"It isn't easy to get a sufficient quantity of pure uranium 235. Even the Americans with all their wealth must have had some difficulty."

"One can well imagine the terrific efforts made by the American scientists. Meanwhile, there must have been many victims, too."

"Of course. There's no progress in science without victims."

"I think they used uranium. Or perhaps they used artificial atoms. It seems that Dr. Fermi of Rome, the highest authority in this field, went to the United States."

"Well, we can't deny that it is a tremendous scientific achievement, this atomic bomb!"

We were members of a research group with a great interest in nuclear physics and totally devoted to this branch of science—and ironically we ourselves had become victims of the atom bomb which was the very core of the theory we were studying. Here we lay, helpless in a dugout!

And yet it was a precious experience for us. Placed on the experimentation table, we could watch the whole process in a most intimate way. We could observe the changes that were taking place and that would take place in the future. Crushed with grief because of the defeat of Japan, filled with anger and resentment, we nevertheless felt rising within us a new drive and a new motivation in our search for truth. In this devastated atomic desert, fresh and vigorous scientific life began to flourish.

7

Atom Bomb Wounds

"Doctor, what's happened? Have I inhaled gas? My whole body somehow feels bad. I'm dizzy as though I was about to collapse."

"Doctor, I must have inhaled the blast from the explosion. I feel nauseous. I can't get up!"

"Doctor, I was buried alive. I wasn't injured and I have no wounds. But today I feel that I'm going to die."

These were the words of people who had fled to the shade of stone walls or to the corners of collapsed buildings and now lay helpless, unable to move.

I myself felt the same way. It was like the awful hangover one experiences after drinking all night at a year-end party. Or, if my readers don't drink, let them recall an experience of violent seasickness and they will understand what I mean. It was an awful feeling of lassitude in the entire body together with headache, nausea, vomiting, dizziness, and loss of energy.

It reminded me of the nauseated feeling I had had when I was exposed to gamma rays while doing radiation experiments. I knew that these people were not sick because they had inhaled gas. Their sickness had nothing to do with the blast from the explosion. It was the effect of gamma rays. At the very instant of the flash, the rays had penetrated their bodies. Moreover, gamma rays can easily pass through the wooden walls of Japanese houses and even comparatively thick concrete walls. Consequently, even people inside houses were affected.

Neutrons also caused severe injuries. I have read about this in scholarly reports, but since I have no direct experience I cannot at this point say whether the sickness here in question was associated with neutron irradiation. Quite certainly, however, severe neutron injury could occur, and since the biological action of neutrons is much more violent than that of gamma rays, it would be very terrible indeed. Moreover, the time when the symptoms appear differs according to the various organs of the body. Each organ has its own period of incubation.

It is awful not to know what symptoms will appear next, or when they will appear. I shuddered to think of the process: atomic bomb . . . neutron irradiation . . . atomic sickness.

The day came to an end with caring for the sick and bringing them to a place of shelter. The next day the sky was bright and cloudless, as the dark atomic cloud veered off to the east. We were caught between the intense heat of the sun and the hot ashes that covered the ground. Urakami was like a oven.

Many of the unfortunate people who on the previous day had fled the tragic scene, escaping from the hands of death and running frantically to the hills, now found that their sanctuary was in fact their last resting place. There they lay in the shade of a rock or a tree, just as they had fallen, unable to move. Some were already dead. Others cried out for water to moisten their lips. Others were just groaning in agony.

Since they had run wildly from the city, not knowing nor caring where they were going, we had no way of finding where they were lying. All we could do was shout out, "Hey! Hey!" and then go wherever there was some response. On Mount Kompira alone there were several hundred, some said several thousand, victims.

Anyhow, the number of wounded was extraordinary. The departments of public health in the prefecture and the city, the association of doctors, and the police—all collaborated to establish a relief service that was efficient and effective. The nearby civilian guard also worked vigorously. The naval hospital at Omura immediately dispatched a relief corps under the command of Dr. Yasuyama. Another detachment arrived from the military hospital in Kurume. Who would have thought that our university, long considered the bastion of medical relief in this region, would be obliged to beg for help? It was sad and humiliating.

However, Professor Koyano, in spite of the fact that his house was burned and his family severely wounded, took on the role of president and became the focus of activity. Professor Cho, who had lost two sons, worked incessantly for the wounded without even searching for the bones of his loved ones. Moreover, the majority of teachers and students, forgetting that they had lost family and property, worked with all their strength to give help, to search for the missing, and to bring order to the confusion that reigned everywhere. President Tsuno and Professor Takagi, lying in the dugout where water was constantly dripping, continued to direct operations while their conditions gradually worsened. Professor Yamane, who was also found badly wounded, was carried in and placed beside them.

The dugout was filling with these serious cases. Enemy planes kept flying overhead. Knowing that another flash would be the end, as soon as we heard the sound of a plane—even if it was far in the distance—we would all rush frantically to the shelter. Our nerves were frayed.

After we had buried the dead and treated the wounded—in so far as that was possible—we were gradually able to put together some observations regarding wounds from the atomic bomb. Some were directly caused by the atomic explosion. Others accompanied the explosion and were indirectly caused by it.

Wounds directly caused by the explosion were the result of pressure, heat, gamma rays, neutrons, and fragments of the bomb (balls of fire). Wounds indirectly caused by the bomb were the result of collapsing houses, flying objects, fire, and the radioactivity given off by objects. And to this second category also belongs temporary insanity arising from shock.

The striking differences between the atom bomb and the usual kind of bomb are: first, in the case of the atom bomb the damage done by flying fragments is insignificant; second, the atomic bomb gives out radioactive rays; third, these radioactive rays continue to do great damage on subsequent days.

The force of the bomb is so terrible that it cannot be expressed in words. People who were fully exposed to it—namely, people who were outside or on the roof of a building or standing at a window —were beaten down or blown away. Those who were within a kilometer of the explosion died instantly or in a few minutes.

Five hundred meters from the explosion lay a mother with her stomach split open while her future baby attached by the umbilical cord dangled between her legs. There were corpses with the belly gaping and the entrails exposed. Seven hundred meters away were heads that had been torn from the trunks of bodies. There were broken skulls with blood dripping from the ears.

Let me say a word about wounds to the skin.

The skin peels off, and it does so instantly. But only that part of the skin burned by the heat peels off from the hypodermic system. It tears away in long strips about a centimeter wide. These rip in the center or at the ends and shrink up, curling slightly inward so that they look like a rag mop or a duster. The color is purplish brown and the part of the skin peeled off shows slight hypodermic bleeding. At the moment of injury, the victim does not feel violent heat but rather momentary acute pain followed by coldness and more intolerable pain. The excoriated skin is very delicate and can easily be cut off. Most of those who sustained this kind of injury died almost immediately.

My conclusion concerning the process of atomic heat wounds is as follows: the exposed parts of the skin are injured by the heat rays. Because of this heat, the dermal system changes, becoming very delicate and fragile. So also does the connective tissue that joins the dermis to the hypodermic system. Since the velocity of the heat rays is thirty million kilometers per second, these rays reach people at the very moment the bomb explodes and bring about the changes I have mentioned. Unexposed parts of the skin, however, do not sustain injury; neither does the connective tissue.

Some time later comes the atomic pressure, followed by the vacuum. When negative pressure is generated around the body, the skin is torn violently outward. The normal skin remains intact; but the burned part is torn off and peels away. This phenomenon is unique and does not occur at any other time.

At a distance of between one and three kilometers from the epicenter, the skin deformation caused by the explosion was the same as in ordinary burns. Some of the victims felt the pain of burning; others felt nothing. Those who felt it spoke of intense heat. The skin immediately became red. Then, after an hour or so, blisters arose.

These burns differed from ordinary burns in that the victims were at the same time penetrated by gamma rays and neutrons. In the future what will happen to these people? This we do not know.

Fragments of the bomb fell like balls of fire. They varied in size. Some were the size of a fingertip, while others were as big as an infant's head. Sending out a bluish white light, they fell with a whistling sound, inflicting lethal wounds on those who were struck by them.

The wounds inflicted on people pinned beneath debris or struck by flying glass and other material, as well as the fate of those who were burned to death in fires—all this was the same as in an ordinary air raid. The only difference was that the area and quantity of destruction brought about in a single moment was incomparably greater.

Inside the narrow dugout we all lay huddled together—the dead, the wounded, and the apparently healthy. When the groaning of a wounded person ceased, we knew that he or she was dead. In the morning we continued our discussion about the atom and about the classification of the dead and wounded. When night fell, we all became silent, utterly exhausted.

In the silence of the night, the horrible scenes of the previous day floated before my eyes one by one. My consciousness flowed into that uneasy borderland between the world of dreams and the world of reality. And all the while, from the ceiling of the dugout, the water kept dripping, dripping as if to measure out time in some uncanny way.

It must have been around midnight when the chief nurse, who had bandaged my head and was now sleeping beside me, suddenly grasped my shoulders in her dream and shouted out: "Oyanagi-san! Oyanagi-san!" This was the name of a nurse who had died the day before.

It was August 11.

In the cool hours of the morning we finally carried all the patients to the military hospital. Now we felt relieved, as though a great burden had been lifted from our shoulders. And having completed our work with the living, we turned to the dead—searching for the bodies of those who were missing and cremating those who were dead. Here and there, sad, red flames arose from the pyres, around which two or three people stood staring vacantly into space.

We buried Yamashita-san and her four companions. But was it possible to bid farewell to these precious lives so simply and without ceremony? On a wooden plaque we made a small inscription in pencil and placed it at the grave. We had no flowers with which to decorate the tomb.

The relatives of students and nurses who had heard of the tragedy and had hurried to the spot were moving here and there amid the debris and calling out names. Whenever they caught a glimpse of someone who resembled the one they sought, they would hurry forward. Sometimes they found a surviving friend of their son or daughter and they would dissolve in tears.

I joined them in their search—pitiful and useless though it was— and shared their tears. Most of them never found the bodies they looked for. Hearing that their son or daughter must have died in such-and-such a classroom, they would go there, pick up some scattered, charred bones, and pray. At other times, when they found a body, the face was so mutilated it was unrecognizable, and they learned the identity only from some small tab sewn to the edge of a garment. Then they stood there stupefied, unable even to weep.

Watercolor by Nagai of a child praying to be reunited in her dreams with her dead mother.

8

Mitsuyama Relief Center

To the north of Nagasaki lies a beautiful range of blue mountains. On the map this mountain range is called Kurodake, but the people simply call it Mitsuyama, meaning "three mountains."

Behind this range lies a valley with a mineral spring famous from antiquity for its healing qualities, particularly for its healing of burns. It is called the water of Koba Rokumai Ita, and from around the Taisho era a small hot-spring inn was located there. Thinking that bathing in the mineral waters would be particularly valuable for healing the innumerable wounds inflicted by the bomb, we set up a first-aid station there in Koba.

And so, on August 12, carrying in our arms the bones of the dead, we left Urakami and made our way to the valley of Mitsuyama. Making a complete break with the world of ashes, we now found ourselves in a different world. What a change it was! The sky was blue like a precious stone and the surrounding world vibrated with life. From time to time we would pause to breathe deeply and expel from our lungs the dust of war. With each deep breath I felt my whole body cleansed through and through. Coming to the Fuji-no-o section of Koba, we borrowed a house and turned it into a first-aid station.

But before doing anything else, we all wound our way through the wood in front of the house and went down to the mountain stream that was flowing in the valley. Leaving our clothes on the rocks, we immersed ourselves in the crystal clear water and let the urgent flood pour over our weary bodies. The rocks were our pillows; the water was our quilt. As we lay back, just as we were, looking up at the sky, both banks rose steeply on either side while the trees crossed their green branches above us. The chorus of cicadas was like falling rain while, in the narrow strip of blue above, fragments of white cloud floated here and there.

I'm alive! I'm alive! I recalled a poem I had composed at the front:

> Today again I have survived;
> I contemplate and relish
> The precious jewel of life.

I repeated the poem again and again.

Getting out of the water, I began to dry myself, and, to my astonishment, I saw that the right side of my body was covered with innumerable little cuts caused by flying glass. Now that I observed them they began to give me pain. I washed my blood-stained clothes and spread them out on the rocks to dry and went to sleep in the shade of a green tree. For the first time since the explosion I experienced the joy of deep sleep.

When I awoke, I heard the nurses lightly snoring. They must have been exhausted.

That evening we went from house to house, visiting the sick and treating their wounds.

We first visited Okumura-san, the head of the village, only to find him lying in bed with serious injuries. It was impossible, he said, to calculate the number of wounded who had fled from the city and had come to these houses.

Next we went to the house of the good farmer Takami-san.

"More than a hundred people, fleeing from Nagasaki, have taken refuge in this house," said his wife as she wiped the sweat from her brow and sliced ten or eleven pumpkins for our meal. Many of the wounded were from Junshin High School—the principal himself was there—and they were sleeping under mosquito nets. One by one they were dying. As for Takami-san, today as every day, he had gone out in the morning to dig graves. And he was still absent.

The wounded had been carried from the scene of the explosion just as they were and had received no medical treatment whatever. Someone had simply covered their injuries with any piece of cloth that was at hand. Many of the wounds were already festering, and, as we removed the makeshift bandages which were sticking to the flesh, the pus poured out with a nauseating stench. When, somewhat crudely, we had washed a wound and cleansed the surrounding area and looked into the affected part, we found bits of concrete or pieces of glass and wood from sliding doors. Accustomed though we were to nauseating scenes, we shuddered at this sight.

One person sometimes had as many as ten or twenty such wounds. This was shocking enough. But the most afflicted person had no less than one hundred and ten. To treat one patient— to wash the wounds, to remove the bits of debris, to sew, to apply medicine, to bandage—all this took time.

The burns also were an ugly sight. Big slices of skin had peeled off, exposing the quivering flesh in an extremely painful way. Most of these burns were on the face, the breast, or the arms. Sometimes the face was so swollen that the person looked like a monster and could scarcely speak. In some cases the patient had been treated with oil according to the usual medical instructions, and then everything had gone well; but in many cases someone had applied crushed potatoes or the rind of pumpkins or even earth; and the result was horrible. We had to disinfect such wounds and order the patient to use hot compresses in the mineral waters of Rokumai Ita.

Finishing our work in one house, we made our way across the field to the next. Whenever we saw a mosquito net, we knew that a wounded person was waiting, and on we moved with courage and endurance.

At ten o'clock in the evening we had completed our visits to the houses of Inutsugi, and, taking care to avoid dangerous vipers, we took the mountain path back to our center at Fuji-no-o. The grass was already covered with dew and choirs of insects filled the valley with song. In the sky the Plow had already fallen, while above Mitsuyama the Scorpion appeared in all its splendor. On the previous night Antares, as I had seen it from my place amidst the atomic rubble of the dugout, had been quivering with an ominous red light; but tonight, as I looked at the same star from the tranquil valley, a sense of intimate kinship arose in my heart.

And so we trudged along in silence. Before my eyes, one by one, floated the faces of my dead colleagues. With affection I also thought of the surviving companions who walked by my side on this mountain path. Once again I raised my eyes to the sky, looking for the Virgin Star far away on the horizon. I wanted to see that blue, clear light and to pray for the repose of those nurses who had died with such beauty in Nagasaki.

August 13 was again cloudless and hot.

At six in the morning we went down to the valley, washed our faces in the stream, and set out for Rokumai Ita. On this one day we planned to visit four villages: Rokumai Ita, Toppomizu, Akamizu, and Odorise. Since this meant a journey of eight kilometers, we wanted to finish the first village before breakfast. But on arriving there, we found the number of wounded far greater than we had anticipated. News that a relief team had come traveled rapidly and people came from all directions. Consequently, our work took us until ten o'clock in the morning.

At the house of the good farmer Matsushita-san, we found quite unexpectedly that breakfast was prepared for us. When we had washed our hands we were welcomed royally. "Please! Come this way!" We were surprised and awed.

As I sat on the tatami mat and took in my fingers the white, steaming rice that was set before me, my eyes filled with tears. "I'm alive! . . . I'm alive! . . . I'm alive!"

"Eat plenty," said our host. "We want you to have energy to help the people in our villages. Eat two meals: breakfast and lunch!" And thus encouraged we all ate a hearty breakfast and went on our way.

We had completed our work in Akamizu and were about to leave when again we heard the fearful sound of an airplane engine. Quickly we scrambled to the shelter of a rock. If there was an atomic flash, it was the end. "No flash! Please, no flash!" I prayed. If it was an ordinary bomb, or there was strafing by machine gun, one could escape unless caught unawares. But against this awful atomic flash there was no defense. No one could foresee where or when it would come. If the flash came, then everything within a radius of several kilometers would be destroyed. No wonder we trembled with fear.

But it did not come. The noise of the engine receded into the distance. We returned to the path and continued on our way.

We marched cautiously in single file, taking care not to cast our dark, flickering shadows on the road where they would be most visible. We were a group of people whose homes had been burned, whose lodging had been burned. We had nowhere to live; we had no clothes to wear; we had lost our loved ones; we had no one to take care of us. We looked just like we did when we left the scene of atomic destruction. And now we were making our rounds, attending to the sick.

Who would have guessed that we were a group of professors, associate professors, nurses, and students—members of the medical faculty of a university? Our heads were wrapped in bandages, and some of those bandages were stained with new blood. Some among us were limping along on wounded legs. Some were wounded in the chest and could scarcely breathe. Others were deathly pale from radioactive injuries. Yet others had lost their glasses and were groping and stumbling on their way. Some were leaning on sticks; others were supporting themselves on the shoulder of a friend. Others again were receiving a helping hand. Some were wearing straw sandals; some wore wooden clogs; some were tripping along in ill-fitting rubber boots. Some wore bloodstained skirts; others had torn shirts or ragged trousers. There were headbands, handkerchiefs, steel helmets. And we all covered our shoulders with green leaves to serve as camouflage against enemy planes.

"What a pitiful sight!" groaned Choro.

"If only things were normal. . . ," sighed young Nagai.

Yes, we were a defeated army in retreat, but even so we were still the faculty of a university. We were dedicated to the truth. We were determined to come to the assistance of the needy, using all our resources. In the heat and the din, searching for the wounded, it was still the pursuit of truth that gave our lives meaning. While this remained vibrant in our hearts, even if our exterior circumstances were wretched, we had no problems.

For the first time in history the atom had exploded over the heads of human beings. Whatever symptoms might appear, the fact was that the patients we were now treating had diseases that were completely new in the annals of medical history. To ignore these patients would not only be an act of cruelty toward individual persons, it would be an unforgivable crime against science, a neglect of precious research material for the future. We ourselves were already experiencing in our bodies the first stirrings of atomic sickness. If we continued our rounds without adequate rest, our symptoms would get worse and worse—and we would die. Or even if we didn't die, we would certainly fall seriously ill.

And yet my academic conscience gave strength to my body. "Examine the patients!" it said. "Observe them carefully! Grasp the evidence! Discover the very best method of treatment!"

Such was the constant inspiration I received from my conscience. We had no machines for making experiments, no instruments to make tests. We had no paper and we had even lost our pencils.

We had only some scalpels and pincettes, some needles and a reserve of disinfectants and bandages which we divided out in bags as medical kits. But we had our heads, our eyes, and our hands. With these we would surely achieve something.

"Enemy planes! Get down! Get down!"

We all dived into the long grass and breathed its fragrance at close quarters. Ants were crawling on the stalks that touched our faces.

"All clear! Back to the road!"

We staggered to our feet and hurried on. The hot sun blazed down on us.

"Enemy planes again! A fighter plane! Get behind that rock! . . . Don't break the medicine bottles! We don't have any more!"

Taking shelter, running, resting our weary bodies in the shade of a tree, looking at our watches unable to believe that so much time had passed, walking on the pebbled road and feeling acute pain from blisters on our feet—this was our way of life. We moved from village to village. But it took more time and energy than we had anticipated. We became exhausted in mind and body.

The wounded were five times more numerous than we had expected. They were in every house. The people who lived in the houses told us that sometimes complete strangers came running up and collapsed before them on the ground. Others, having nowhere to go, had spread mats in bamboo thickets and were lying there.

We ran out of bandages. The chief nurse and Tsubakiyama volunteered to make the hour's journey along that charred road down to the university. "If there's another flash, we meet in heaven," we said, half-joking and half-serious, as we embraced them and watched them make their way down the valley.

When evening came they appeared—how anxiously we had been waiting—with joyful faces and with bags of bandages. With them came Nurse Oishi. She had received news that her brother had been killed in action and on August 9 she had returned to her home in Kita Matsuura. That same day she heard about the destruction of the university and so she hurried back, hoping that she could help her companions and professors. "At least I wanted to greet the bones of my professors," she exclaimed with tears running down her cheeks.

With the additional help of the energetic Nurse Oishi, our work went on briskly. By ten o'clock in the evening we had done all the villages we had set out to visit that day and we returned to Fuji-no-o.

We lit a fire in the hearth and boiled sweet potatoes and pumpkins. Sitting around the fire, we discussed the symptoms of the various patients we had treated. It now became clear that the most serious injuries from radioactive rays were to the digestive system. Around the mouth appeared pustular eruptions, and there was inflammation within the mouth. These were symptoms we had never seen before. Throwing pieces of wood on the flames, we entered into heated discussion, and before we knew it the sweet potatoes and the pumpkins were steaming hot and giving off a delicious smell.

August 14. Today four villages to visit: Azebetto, Kawadoko, Tobita, and Kotani. In all, a journey of nine kilometers.

The road zigzagged across mountains and through valleys, linking the houses that were scattered between.

"There's a house on top of that mountain!"

Instinctively our legs resist. But there might be a sick person in the house. How can we run away? And so, putting strength into these hands that grasp our sticks, we climb the mountain step by step.

We found the families overflowing with joy at our arrival. The wounded, thinking that they would certainly receive help now that some doctors had come to treat them, began to use their disabled hands to remove bandages. From the kitchen came the sound of a knife chopping cucumbers—ton! ton! ton! When our work was completed we would eat with our hosts.

And so we trudged from village to village on our pilgrimage to help the wounded, to bring joy to the families, to further the progress of medical science. When the evening sun became a ball of red fire, we were hungry, exhausted, overcome with pain, ready to collapse. Two by two, grasping one another's hands, we returned in silence along that mountain path lit by the evening sun.

Suddenly Choro broke wind with a long, loud rasp.

"Ho! Ho! Ho!" laughed the chief nurse as she ran ahead.

"Isn't he horrible!" exclaimed Little Bean.

"It's O.K. It's O.K.," said Choro nonchalantly. "This is a rocket launching pad." And again he broke wind. But this time the sound wasn't as good.

"The hydrogen peroxide isn't pure," laughed young Nagai, teasing him.

"The machine is all right, but there's not enough fuel," retorted Choro.

And then with a laugh, and without even noticing the distance, we continued on our way.

The evening moon was shining faintly.

"It's already late and the way is long," murmured Professor Seiki.

And just at that moment a spasm of pain shot through my right leg, the leg that had been giving me trouble for some time. It was a cramp, and I doubled up in pain on the ground. My companions rushed to my side and began to massage the leg vigorously. The moon was gradually falling and it became dark all around. No one passed by. We still had three kilometers to go before reaching Fuji-no-o. But when thirty minutes had passed, the muscles of my leg became soft again and, supporting myself on the shoulder of Little Bean, I dragged my feet along the way.

But we had scarcely gone one kilometer when Little Bean herself became weak and collapsed. And so Little Barrel and Nurse Oishi locked their arms and carried her, while Choro took me on his back.

At last we reached the house of Takami-san and were able to breathe freely. "Dear me, you're so late!" exclaimed the woman of the house; and she immediately set the evening meal in front of us. We hadn't the courage even to demur. Choking and coughing like little dogs, we shoved in rice, pumpkins, sweet potatoes, and plums.

August 15. Feast of the Assumption of the Virgin Mary.

Mass was celebrated at dawn in the church of Koba. But the roar of enemy planes sweeping across the sky forced us to interrupt the service. Father Shimizu quickly carried the Eucharist to the shelter at the back of the church.

After mass we immediately set out for the village of Inutsugi to continue our medical treatment. Today we felt that we were reaching the limits of our endurance. Indeed, we began to think that we might be the most serious cases of all. While the patients were able to talk, we had to pause and reflect before answering.

People continued to die. It seemed to be the crisis day for the wounded. "It's a war! Stick it out!" we said as we encouraged one another and kept working.

Early in the morning Choro had gone to the main building of the university to replenish our food supplies. Toward evening he returned. He had been hurrying and was out of breath. He opened the bags of rice and the packets of bean paste and took out the canned foods. We gave him a great welcome. And then what news fell from his lips!

"It looks as if the war is over," he said.

"And the conditions?" we asked.

"Unconditional surrender. Total acceptance of the Potsdam Declaration."

For a moment there was a deathly silence.

"It's a lie," I said.

"There's terrific confusion in the town," Choro went on. "Some are insisting that it's a lie. Others say it's true. At noon there was an important announcement by radio. There was so much jamming or atmospherics that I couldn't hear properly. But the word *'Chin,'* reserved for the emperor himself, kept coming through. Some people said it was the voice of His Majesty himself. But the military police kept driving around the town in trucks, shouting that the noon broadcast was a trick of the enemy and we shouldn't believe it. They said we would fight to the end—even on our own soil. Several people who said the war was over were beaten up by young men standing nearby."

Gloom descended on our group. Again we lapsed into silence and turned our attention to the wounded.

Was it true? No. It must be a lie. It must be a false rumor. But no, it might be the truth. It was as though a truck were whirling around inside my head.

When we finished our work and washed our hands it was again ten o'clock in the evening. We made a simple meal from the cans that Choro had carried up from the town. Our stomachs were empty; but the food had no taste.

August 16.

An atomic time bomb has fallen . . . a small uranium bomb with a clock-like mechanism. It is ticking, ticking, ticking. After five minutes it will explode. But no one knows it has fallen here. I become wild and flurried. I must destroy this thing. Fortunately I'm holding a bamboo spear. "Eh!" I shout as I stab at the bomb with the spear. But the spear doesn't penetrate and bends. Beside me are a number of bamboo spears. Taking one more I make a thrust forward; but this atom bomb is a stubborn fellow and the spear bends and breaks. Now I become irritated, then angry. "Eh! Ya! . . . Eh! Ya! . . ." I shout as I make yet another thrust with the spear. My breathing becomes painful; sweat breaks out all over my body. The bomb will certainly explode. I'm trembling with fear. The rumbling sound has begun. Now the awful flash of light! The rays are striking my face. "It's all over!" I scream.

"Doctor! Doctor! What's the matter?"

The face of the chief nurse appeared above me as I opened my eyes. Little Bean opened the shutters and a stream of sunlight fell on my face.

"Dear, dear! You have a fever," said the chief nurse as she placed her hand on my forehead and wiped away the sweat with a towel.

I tried to get up but was overcome with dizziness. I noticed that there was pain in my right leg and I could not move it. The chief nurse was examining the leg. "All your wounds are festering. Why did you let things go so far without saying anything?" she said, scolding me. "It's a war," I said undaunted. But I knew I would not be able to get up that day.

They began to treat my wounds and give me injections. Then they set out for Kawahira. Tsubakiyama went down to the town to get some reliable news. I was left alone with my groaning to look after the place while they were gone.

"Doctor!" said a voice. It was Tsubakiyama, back from the town. With a dark, sad face she gave me the newspaper.

With a single glance I saw the whole story. These were words I never wanted to see. For years I had fought and struggled not to see them:

By a sacred imperial decree the war is over.

Japan was defeated! Raising my voice, I began to weep. The tears overflowed and I covered my ears. For twenty minutes, for thirty minutes I wept like a child. When my tears dried, my sobbing would not stop. Tsubakiyama was lying on the tatami matting convulsed with tears, her shoulders shaking as she sobbed.

Early in the evening our companions who had gone out on relief work returned. Seeing their faces, I again broke down in torrential tears. We all held hands and wept. On and on it went. The sun set and the moon rose; but we could not stop weeping. There we sat without touching our meal, without drinking our tea, without thinking of anything, without saying a word. Our faces, white as milk, sank into a sea of tears. When there were no more tears to shed, the day's fatigue rose to the surface and we fell into a deep sleep.

August 17.

Empires crumble, but the mountains and rivers remain.

Opening the sliding doors, I looked at the mountains. The three peaks of Mitsuyama were tranquil as ever. They did not even seem to notice the fragments of cloud that floated beneath their towering heights. All things pass. All things are like a fragment of cloud. Our faith in the eternal stability of the Japanese Empire had crumbled in a moment.

In the clear blue sky of the morning, American planes circled victoriously round and round just as they pleased. First came a Grumman. Then a Lockheed. All flew low in the sky at a leisurely speed as though wanting to take a good look at the ground beneath. A B-29 appeared. Its huge body seemed almost to touch the three peaks of Mitsuyama. Then it flew away.

The war was over and we were defeated. Today we would simply spend sleeping and doing nothing. After breakfast we lay on our mats looking at the clouds, looking at the trees, looking at the planes. We felt like doing nothing. Cups and plates lay at the hearth, unwashed and abandoned.

A man arrived asking us to visit a wounded person.

"Japan has lost. Why talk about the wounded? There are a hundred million people today in tears. Are we to make a fuss about the life or death of one or two of them? Even if we do help them, will it make any difference? Japan will never rise again. . . . Refuse!" And I curtly refused our help.

Today we were sick and irritable. The slightest thing would make us fight and quarrel.

"I see," said the man lifelessly. And he walked away, dejected and sad.

From my place on the mat I watched him intently as he crossed the field in front of the house and was about to disappear from sight.

Then I suddenly jumped to my feet and told Little Bean to call him back. In a flash I had had a change of heart. Even one precious life was worth saving. Japan was defeated; but the wounded were still alive. The war was over; but the work of our relief team remained. Our country was destroyed; but medical science still existed. Wasn't our work only beginning? Irrespective of the rise and fall of our country, wasn't our main duty to attend to the life and death of each single person? The very basis of the Red Cross was to attend to the wounded, be they friend or foe. Precisely because we Japanese had treated human life so simply and so carelessly—precisely for this reason we were reduced to our present miserable plight. Respect for the life of every person—this must be the foundation stone on which we would build a new society.

Our people had been told that they must suffer these terrible wounds to win the war; but in fact they had suffered in order to lose. Now they were thrown into the most pitiable and desperate situation. And there was no one to console them, no one to help them except us. We must stand and come to their aid. I stood there unsteadily on my tottering legs. And then the whole group stood up beside me. Our courage came back. The determination to continue our work gave us strength and joy.

"It's a war!" With these words we had been forced to fight on and on. With these words we had been forced to do anything and everything without reasoning or questioning. But such words would no longer move us. Now we saw that no one but us could save this precious life, and we would move spontaneously forward to help and to serve. Of course our bodies were utterly exhausted;

but we would not neglect the wounded, even when our own wounds hurt us at every step.

A fighter plane with clear American markings flew down low over our heads. Today nothing would happen even though we looked pretty numerous as we trudged along the road. Whenever an American plane flew overhead we felt a strange sense of relief that we need not run for shelter.

August 18. The rumor spread that the Allied forces were landing and that the women must flee to the mountains for safety.

It was a spectacle both sad and humorous to see wealthy Japanese carrying their belongings and running here and there in panic. For a few weeks after the surrender the turmoil took various forms, and all around us was confusion.

But we ourselves had no possessions whatever: we had nothing to lose. All we had was a great number of sick and wounded. So we continued calmly on our rounds, bringing relief to those in need.

But we were sad and heavy at heart. Our Japan—the Japan symbolized by Mount Fuji piercing the clouds and enlightened by the sun that rose in the eastern sea—was dead. Our people, the people of Yamato, were cast to the very depths of an abyss. We who were alive lived only in shame. Happy indeed were our companions who had left this world in the holocaust of the atomic bomb.

We lived with a deep inner grief. Every day after supper in the open air beneath the rays of the moon or, when the rain was pattering down on the roof and the mountains and the surrounding world, around the hearth, we would gather and enter into thoughtful discussion. We talked about the future. Where did our path lie? But during the day we were able to transcend all these troubles and concentrate our powers on saving each individual human life.

The dreadful atomic sickness showed itself increasingly in our patients, in the refugees who had once seemed quite healthy, and in ourselves. Certain symptoms were exactly as we had expected from former laboratory experiments. Indeed, we almost felt proud that they confirmed our theories so well. But other symptoms arose suddenly and unexpectedly so that we were deeply perplexed.

In this way we continued our relief work at Mitsuyama for two months; that is, until October 8.

One by one the members of our team collapsed into sick-beds. Atom bomb wounds, overwork, and undernourishment had sapped our strength in a dangerous way. Professor Fuse's white corpuscles were reduced to half the normal count. Moriuchi began to hemorrhage. The chief nurse lost her hair. Those who collapsed absented themselves from the rounds and lay writhing in pain.

Meanwhile their companions, returning from the villages, spent the night caring for them; and when dawn broke they again made their customary rounds from village to village and from house to house, trudging through the blazing hot valley for a distance of about eight kilometers each day. When, after some time, the people lying in bed recovered and were able to get up, their companions who had nursed them collapsed with high fever.

To show and to receive tender care, to give and to receive injections—this was our life. When someone said that he or she was thirsty, another would go down to the stream in the valley and, scooping up clear water, bring it back. Or if someone could not eat the food, another would give him or her a couple of pears received at a patient's house. To get medicine for injections some of our group traveled all the way to Nagasaki and back by the mountain road—a distance of about twenty-five kilometers.

On September 20, I myself fell seriously ill and abandoned all hope of life. Symptoms of atomic sickness had appeared and a high fever continued for a week.

And just at that time a request for help came from Kida, a village on top of the mountain. I knew that if I went I would probably die but, thinking that to offer my life for one unknown person would be a worthwhile sacrifice, I set out on the journey. My legs trembled beneath me. On the way I stopped to rest at the shelter of the Jun-shin Convent at Kawadoko. "I can't understand! I can't under-stand why you overtax your strength in this way!" said the superior scoldingly. But I succeeded in treating the wounded person. And then, arriving home late at night, I collapsed into bed like a stone falling into the valley—never to rise again.

When I awoke painfully from my unconscious state, I noticed something strange about my breathing. Anxiously attending to my body, I recognized the symptoms of Cheyne-Stokes respiration. This is a special kind of breathing that begins a few hours before death.

"Cheyne-Stokes," I said aloud.

Beside my bed sat Dr. Tomita, a former research student in our department. He had been called to the front and now, quite unex-pectedly, had returned.

"Yes," he said with an embarrassed look.

"You've come a long way, Doctor," I said, extending my hand in welcome. "I'm sorry to be so much trouble."

Just then Morita-san, the head nurse at the military hospital, appeared. "It's all right, Dr. Nagai," she said firmly. "Just be quiet." And with that she gave me an injection in the arm. Judg-ing from the pain, it must have been coramine. My pulse was also weak and I felt a disturbing and agonizing pain in my chest—as though an empty car were lurching around inside me. But the nurse had said everything would be all right, so it would be all right. Yet I could not move my head. I could not even open my eyes. Somehow I felt that a great number of people had gathered and they were whispering to one another and there was a lot of com-motion.

"Where is Dr. Fuse?" I asked weakly.

"He's away just now. But he'll soon be back," said the chief nurse.

"I see," I said. And with that I became unconscious.

Little did I know that Dr. Fuse, desperately anxious to help me, had talked with Professor Cho, had pleaded with Professor Kageura, had visited Professor Koyano. From morning till evening he had been running around trying to get the information and the medicine that would help me. But all the doctors who heard about my symptoms had concluded that there was no hope. When I fell into this coma, without my knowing it, many friends had hurried to my side and gathered around my bed. They had all made sacrifices to save my life.

Father Tagawa came and I prepared myself for the end. I believe I would have been happy to die then. But death did not come.

When I opened my eyes and came out of the coma, it looked like afternoon. Seeing my friends around my bed, a thrill of happiness pervaded my being. My heart was causing me acute pain. I knew that if another cramp came I would die.

The sliding doors were open and from where I lay I could see the three peaks of Mitsuyama. Rising calmly into that clear sky, they were a symbol of the Holy Trinity. Autumn had begun.

The sparkling autumn cloud
Rises high in the sky
And disappears from sight.

Twice I repeated these words and then lapsed into my last coma.

A week later I emerged from unconsciousness. Everyone called it a miracle.

What deep friendship, what union, what intimacy bound us together in those difficult days!

In the evening, by the light of the lantern and amidst the chorus of insects, we prayed for the repose of our dead companions. If we received some persimmons from Takimi-san, we thought of the sparkling eyes of Inoue. If Harada-san gave us rice cakes for the village festival, we thought of Hama. If the wife of the basket maker gave us winter cherries for the house altar, the red nose of Yamashita floated before our eyes. If we got potatoes from Matsushita-san, we lamented that Oyanagi and Yoshida should have gone through the potato field just at that time. Tears rose to our eyes when we considered how happy we would be if only Fujimoto and Kataoka and Kosasa were enjoying this meal with us.

9

Atom Bomb Sickness

A good deal of research concerning the effects of radiation from nuclear fission on living things had already been done in clinical tests and experiments with different kinds of animals before the atomic bomb exploded. Although the reaction is different between a large amount of radiation released over a short period of time and a small amount over a long period, radiation always has a destructive effect on tissue cells.

When exposed to radiation, tissue begins to deteriorate. However, the effect does not appear at once, and each internal organ has its own latent period. The person may not feel any pain or may not be aware of being injured at the time of irradiation. When radiation penetrates the human body, it does not stimulate the nervous system, so the person does not even know that he or she has been irradiated until the symptoms appear some time later.

Some organs are highly resistant to radiation while others are very sensitive to it. The bone marrow, the lymph glands, and the generative glands are the weakest and can sustain great injuries.

The bone marrow produces blood cells. Thus when it is injured, both white and red blood cells will be diminished. When the degree of injury is high, the bone marrow will change and will continuously send unfinished white cells into the blood. This increase of abnormal white blood cells causes the disease leukemia. In particular, when a small amount of radiation is received over a long period of time, leukemia is easily contracted.

The tonsils—a lymph gland—are very susceptible to radiation and frequently die.

When the generative glands are injured, the result is loss of sexual energy, deficiency in the production of sperm, a cessation of menstruation, and sterility. There can be stillbirths and births of deformed children. The breasts also become small.

The next weakest is the mucous membrane. When this is injured, congestion and inflammation result. In extreme cases, ulcers are formed.

When the digestive organs' mucous membrane is injured, one contracts stomatitis, gastritis, and intestinal inflammation. This leads to dysentery-like diarrhea. Moreover, the papillae at the roots of the hair are damaged and the hair begins to fall out. But this can be cured, and the hair begins to grow again. The lungs develop pneumonia and the kidneys become atrophied. If the adrenal gland is injured, the skin becomes dark.

One example of a symptom affecting the entire body is radiation nausea, which appears a few hours after exposure and lasts for a few days. The younger the person the more violent the effect. Young people may die while older people survive.

There is a certain fatal dose for each type of radiation. Since each cell has its own latent period prior to visible appearance of the injury, death does not occur immediately. However, a person irradiated with more than the fatal dose cannot be cured, whatever the treatment. The greater the dose the more violent the symptoms and immediate death may result.

But what sort of symptoms actually appeared as a result of the atomic bomb?

The symptoms were more or less similar to what radiotherapeutics has taught us until now. The radiation operant in the case of the atomic bomb was caused by the neutron and gamma rays flying about at the time of the explosion, and by the radioactivity that remained for a long time in the area away from the wind at the center of the explosion; that is to say, in the eastern region.

Strictly speaking, each of these types of radioactivity was different. By far the most powerful was the neutron. Very troublesome, though much weaker, was the remnant radioactivity. This later was the basis for the theory that the contaminated area would remain uninhabitable for seventy-five years.

When people said they had inhaled gas or that they had been struck by the atomic blast, they actually meant that they had been irradiated. Since people sometimes think that diseases only enter through the mouth, they make this kind of interpretation, saying they have inhaled gas. But in fact radiation can easily penetrate any part of the body and can then have violent effects.

Let me briefly examine the atomic sicknesses caused by the bomb according to the time of their appearance.

About three hours after the explosion, radiation nausea began to be felt and it reached its peak in twenty-four hours. After that it gradually decreased.

Usually on the third day injury to the digestive organs appeared and killed many people in about one week. For those who were slightly affected, diarrhea lasted for some time.

In the second week some people began to hemorrhage. This was caused by circulatory disorders; and many people died. Loss of hair began in the course of the third week. The fourth week brought serious symptoms because of the decrease in white blood cells; and again, many people died. Injury to the generative glands continued to appear for more than ten weeks after the explosion.

On the whole, the symptoms appeared earlier and were more severe in the case of children than of adults.

Even now, at the time of writing, a small quantity of radioactivity remains at the center of the explosion and an increase in white blood cells is noticeable among the inhabitants of this area.

Now let me comment briefly on a few other important points.

I have already spoken about radiation nausea when discussing the wounds caused by the atomic bomb. Our observations of injury to the digestive organs tally exactly with the results of the experiments done with animals. That is to say, there is congestion and ulcerous inflammation of the mucous membrane. Some people who had been buried beneath fallen houses and other debris within one kilometer of the center of the explosion were at first happy to have survived unscathed. But about three days later bean-sized pustules began to appear around their mouths; and on the following day they got stomatitis with intense pain. Then they experienced great difficulty in eating and drinking. Their temperature went up and they lost appetite. More stomach pains and diarrhea followed. Symptoms of intestinal inflammation appeared. At first the diarrhea was liquid but by degrees mucous was mixed with it. Later, blood appeared. The body temperature mounted to 40° Centigrade and some of the cases were mistakenly diagnosed as dysentery. They became very weak and died within a week or ten days. Others, however, who were slightly injured complained only of diarrhea and loss of appetite.

As I have said, certain traces of radioactivity remained. Some people got diarrhea just from passing through Urakami during the first ten days after the explosion.

Some deaths, but not many, occurred from hemorrhage during the second week. Sudden nosebleeding, vomiting of blood, bloody diarrhea, and new bleeding of old wounds occurred, causing death. The blood platelet in the venous blood was destroyed and there arose a tendency to bleeding. Experiments have been made with rabbits on this point.

With the coming of September and the cool weather, the confusion after the capitulation died down. Patients now began to have hope that they would live.

However, toward September 5—four weeks after the explosion—serious symptoms of disorder in the white blood cells suddenly appeared. People began to die in rapid succession. This threw everybody into a state of acute fear and panic. It happened this way.

Many people living in houses within a distance of one kilometer from the explosion—people who had suffered from nothing worse than slight diarrhea and had been devoting themselves to the service of others—suddenly fell ill. There were, at first, warning symptoms. There was fatigue in the whole body, while the skin turned white. Next the temperature mounted higher than 40° Centigrade and stayed at that level for some time. Then they got stomatitis with tooth gum ulcers leading to the death of the gums. They could neither eat nor drink on account of roughening of the laryngeal membrane and ulcerous tonsilitis. Purplish red spots then began to appear on the skin—first on the trunk and on the upper arms and later on the thighs. Their size grew from that of a pin to that of a rice grain, to that of a bean and eventually they became as large as a fingertip. Yet the victims felt neither pain nor itching. Finally the white blood cells diminished greatly; and those with less than two thousand could not be saved. The process was quite rapid and they died in about nine days.

Indirect radiation injury was less common. But let me give one example.

The grass, the trees, and whatever grew within two to seven kilometers—all were irradiated at the time of the explosion and burned red. Moreover, the leaves on which the big drops of black rain fell withered and died.

The day after the explosion, two farmers cut down some of the dead miscanthus and carried it on their shoulders. And the next day their arms, legs, and shoulders, which had been touched by the dead leaves, got itching red edema. It looked like skin poisoning but it disappeared in a few days.

But what about the influence of residual radioactivity? What about people who were not in Urakami at the time of the explosion and consequently were not injured, people who were not exposed to the flash but came to live at the center of the explosion? In order to study these cases I closed the Mitsuyama relief station and built myself a hut in Ueno-cho at the center of the explosion, where I now live. I have carefully observed the surrounding area up to the present.

Immediately after the explosion, the existence of substantial radioactivity was demonstrated. The element that was the source of this radioactivity was the new atom produced by nuclear fission. At first it floated in the sky as a mushroom cloud; but eventually it fell to earth, taking the form of extremely minute dust that by itself was not visible to the eye.

At the time of the division of the uranium, radioactive barium and strontium were produced. In addition, the powerful radiation from the explosion caused the atoms in matter on the ground to undergo fission—and some may have become temporarily radioactive.

However, all these radioactive substances will gradually regain stability in their atoms and will lose radioactivity. Some have already been washed away by water, and the radioactive counts at the central zone of the explosion decrease every day. Yet even now—one year after the explosion—a small amount still remains and continues in a weak manner its work of irradiation.

From what I have said it will be clear that the effect of radiation on the human body was more violent at the beginning. The district of Ueno where I now live lies within six hundred meters of the center. All the inhabitants were killed except one child who was hidden deep inside a shelter. Indeed, the area became a heap of ash and rubble.

Those who came to live here within three weeks of the explosion began gradually to experience nausea and injury to the digestive organs. This lasted for more than a month. They also suffered from severe diarrhea. The condition of people who dug among the ashes in order to take away the remains of burned houses, or who carried tiles, or who looked after the bodies of the dead—their condition was the worst. Their symptoms resembled those of people who had been profoundly irradiated during the explosion itself. No doubt this was the effect of heavy and continuous residual irradiation on their entire bodies.

The condition of people who moved into the place after one month was better. Nevertheless, nausea and injury to the digestive organs was much in evidence. Pus formed easily on mosquito bites, flea bites, or any small injury. Moreover, the number of white blood cells seemed to decrease.

After three months no more obvious symptoms of any injury appeared. People began to move in and to build houses. These were mostly demobilized soldiers, evacuees, and repatriates.

And yet, examining the white blood cells, one could observe that one month after moving into the area there was an extraordinary increase—the count doubled. These symptoms were the result of continuous exposure to a small quantity of radioactive rays. In other words, a very tiny amount of radioactivity still remains in this place; and that is exactly as the Americans warned us at the time of the explosion. But since the speed of decrease in radioactivity is rather rapid, the seventy-five-years theory is not tenable. It seems to me that the danger from radioactivity will not continue for long. At present the health of the inhabitants is good, even though the white blood cells have increased. Although I have lived here for some time I have never been asked to examine patients except in cases of parasitic diseases.

I myself sleep in a small hut with icicles hanging on the walls and roof and with snow filtering in. I have only a thin blanket to protect me. And yet I have not contracted pneumonia, nor even so much as a cold. Even if I get an injury or scratch I have no fear of infection or of pus developing in the wounds. Indeed, I feel like an inhabitant of a radium hot-spring region.

What concerns me most is injury to the generative glands. How-ever, I see that some young wives are already pregnant, even though the rate of pregnancy seems to have diminished somewhat. We do not hear of stillbirths, and no deformed babies have been born. Although we should be slow to make predictions about the future, I am rather optimistic and am persuading people to return to the ruins and rebuild their houses.

Another subject of concern at present is the prognosis for burns on the skin. These severe burns have been caused not only by intense heat but also by irradiation from both neutrons and gam-ma rays. Indeed, they are quite different from ordinary burns. Even in the case of ordinary burns some people get clubfoot edema, depending on their condition. But of those burned by the atomic explosion almost all got clubfoot edema.

In the city of Nagasaki one often meets people whose faces and hands are pink and shining and swollen. These are symptoms of clubfoot edema. If one is injured by radiation leading to clubfoot edema, the skin itches and, if one continues to scratch, after a few years one might get an ulcer; and still many years later one might get cancer. This has frequently been shown in the case of radium and X-ray irradiation.

Does the injury stemming from atom bomb burns result in cancer? This is the most serious problem remaining for the future. Those who have sustained such injuries must be careful not to scratch the skin. After taking a bath they should not rub the in-jured part and they should avoid using just any kind of medicine.

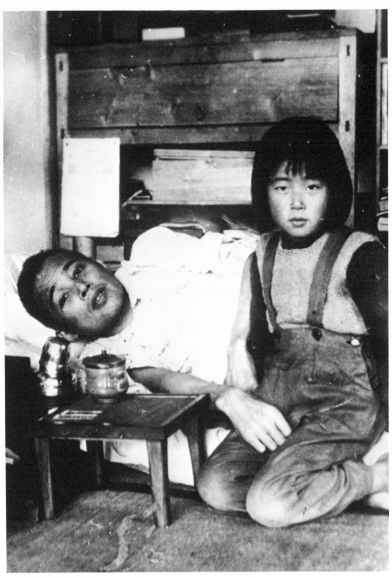

Nagai and Kayano.

10

Atomic Sickness Therapy

Injection of vitamin B and grape sugar was very effective in counteracting nausea.

For burns, mineral water therapy was far better than anything else. We divided the patients into two groups: the first group received mineral water therapy and the second group ordinary therapy with medicine. And we watched the healing process.

The first group took an average of only twenty days for total healing, while the second took thirty-eight days. That is to say, those who took mineral water therapy were healed, on an average, two weeks earlier. Bathing in mineral water is good for any external injury; and I myself have profited greatly from it.

We were the first doctors to give atom bomb patients the so-called shock therapy with the patient's own blood. This therapy has spread rapidly and widely; we asked all the doctors to follow it. I myself think it is extremely effective, but since the opinions of doctors who used it vary considerably, the last word has not yet been said. All we can say is that many doctors found it beneficial. This therapy had been used for other patients, but on September 10 Dr. Fuse tried it on atomic bomb patients for the first time. Here is how it came about.

At the beginning of September many people suddenly became seriously ill with symptoms of subcutaneous hematoma: high fever, death of tooth gum, and throat ulcers. We began to wonder if this was septicemia or some new epidemic disease. But as we watched closely, giving symptomatic treatment, we realized that there were similarities to granulocyte deficiency, which is a disease of the blood. We eventually found that the symptoms were caused by a decrease in white blood cells due to injury to the bone marrow by irradiation.

The patients died in rapid succession. Led by Dr. Fuse, we all tended them night and day, meanwhile trying our utmost to find a suitable therapy. And it was at this time that we came theoretically to the conclusion that shock treatment with the patient's own blood would be effective.

We acted at once. Taking 2 cc of the patient's blood, we injected it into his or her hip muscle. The results were good. The dying patients were all saved. Indeed, after our discovery of this therapy no more deaths from this disease occurred.

As for nutrition, a form of liver-and-vegetable food therapy was adopted. The liver of any animal was given; if possible it was given raw or only slightly cooked. The patient was also fed a lot of vegetables. And this was quite successful.

Rice wine, or *sake*, proved to be an excellent medicine. There were examples of dying persons being cured at the last moment by drinking a large quantity of their favorite *sake*.

Recuperation at home was excellent for the patients—as became clear in many cases. One cannot imagine how much valuable rest and refreshment patients get—especially in times of chaos and confusion—from recuperating at home among understanding relatives and friends who look after them with loving care. This is much better than spending dreary days feeling ill at ease in some first-aid station.

The daily rounds made by our relief squad to give this treatment were exhausting and burdensome. We didn't receive a cent for our services. Thus, I wanted at least to present each of the nurses with a pair of wooden clogs.

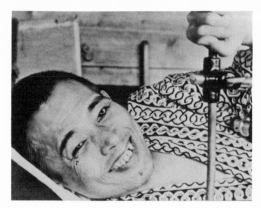

The author, May 1949.

11

Visitors to My Hut

The decision was made to reopen the university. Medical work and research began in the buildings of Shinkozen Public School.

The few other survivors of the bomb gathered together; and we too came down from the valley of Mitsuyama and returned to our university. On November 2, we held a memorial service in which we prayed for the repose of the souls of our 807 dead companions.

I took up residence in a tiny hut of galvanized iron that was made for me at Ueno-cho near the center of the explosion. The back of my hut is a stone wall—extremely practical in that I can store papers and other things in the holes. But when it rains it has its drawbacks. My colleagues call it a box.

All kinds of visitors come. One day it is the bishop. On another day a beggar might drop in. The American military chaplain paid me a visit. "Is this your palace?" he quipped. And while I was receiving a visit from a professor of a distant university, the military authorities sent me an old pair of shoes—a gift for a war victim, they said.

Yamamoto and Hamazato, my former students, returned from the war. They sat before me in silence, without a single word. We knew that if a word were spoken we would burst into tears.

At last they broke the silence.

"Professor, it's a tragedy!"

The author and Kayano meeting
Helen Keller (far left).

"You fought well. Thank you!" I said.

"It's an intolerable situation. We must get our revenge. Even
if it takes ten years, we'll win this war."

"You think it's a tragedy?"

"Yes, we do."

"If we lose a war that we ought to have won, we can say it's
a tragedy or that it's a pity. Or we can use these words when we
still have military power."

"Japan wasn't so weak. We weren't actually defeated. We still
have plenty of military power."

"That's strange! Hasn't Japan surrendered unconditionally? We
realized we had lost all power to fight and we surrendered to the
enemy forces."

"No! I've still got it in me to go on fighting."

"That's even stranger. In fact it's awful. Why didn't Japan use
all her military power before the capitulation? And when our country has lost its power to resist, do you as an individual still retain
such power? The way you talk reminds me of a family that has

100

lost all its money and is on the verge of collapse—and then the young son boasts that he has concealed his money in the bank. . . . Look! During the war I obeyed my country faithfully and I fought with everything I had. Our university also fought with the utmost determination to the very end. In the most savage air raids we went courageously to the rescue of the wounded; we were true to the spirit of the Red Cross. Till the very moment the atomic bomb exploded over our heads, we were prepared to go anywhere at any time to give relief to suffering people. What's more, we were always faithful to the basic mission of a university: to hold our classes and to conduct our medical research. When the university was destroyed by the atomic bomb, we remained firmly at our post, not abandoning the university until we had done all that was humanly possible. Our young people continued their relief work with the utmost dedication and without a trace of cowardice—that's something beautiful, something splendid. And that holds true even if Japan is defeated; even if it is shown that our motive for war was unjust."

"Yes, we agree. Regardless of the fate of our country, it *is* beautiful to see these young people with love for humanity devoting themselves to their duty to the very end."

"The university has lost everything. The buildings are totally destroyed. Most of the staff and students have died, and those of us who survived are crippled and useless as you can see. My wife is dead; my property is lost; my house is destroyed. I've lost everything. I have nothing. I gave everything I had but I was defeated. Why should I say that it's a tragedy or a pitiful situation? Why is it pitiful? Our situation now is like that of a man who looks at the moon after the rain. It was a war. We lost. I have no regrets."

"When you talk that way you make us feel ashamed."

"And I would have felt embarrassed, too; I would have suffered spiritually if the capitulation had come while I still had my wife, my property, and my home. Wouldn't I have felt an intolerable burden when I saw my country in ruins and my compatriots burned out of their homes? But when I reflect that with the destruction of my country I was left homeless and penniless, then in the midst of sadness a fresh spirit, one of joy, rises in me.''

"But before us we have to watch a group of people rejoicing morning and evening because they've profited from the war.''

"Yes. That's true. They're the people who must be crushed. War is a money-making business. These people know that if there is a war once every ten years they'll become millionaires. They are the pigs. And it's lust for money, precisely this, that will be the source of warmongering in the future. This is the gang that seduces our young and innocent people with talk about revenge.''

"They really are pigs, who feed themselves at the expense of the country. . . . But is war a business that really brings profit to the nation?''

"If you win, I suppose it does.''

"But if war is waged to bring profit to the nation, can that war be called just?''

"There can be no victory in a war that is unjust in the eyes of God.''

"But during the war we prayed constantly to God. In particular, we prayed to the god of war.''

"The god of war? He's a man-made god, like the god who heals whooping cough.''

"No. I'm talking about the gods who were in Japan from ancient times.''

"Those gods were created by our ancestors whose knowledge of philosophy and theology was more primitive than ours. They made their gods to suit their purpose and then they asked them for what they wanted. Those were really just paper gods. And in this way we came to believe in the invincibility of our country and in legends about the divine wind and the like. We were paying homage to dead images.''

"Do you think we lacked sincerity?''

"Not at all. But no matter how sincere one is, it's useless to pray to beings that don't exist. We couldn't stand up to people who trusted not in man-made gods but in the true God.''

"But just as we Japanese have our own spirit, the spirit of Yamato, so we should have our own gods.''

"If these gods are freely accepted by the people and not imposed at the point of the sword—yes! But your way of thinking reveals a religion that's no more than a primitive nationalism. It was criticized and judged in Rome two thousand years ago.''

"Let's leave this talk about gods for later. Isn't it said that war is the mother of civilization? Doesn't it give a great stimulus to science? Think, for example, of the atomic bomb!''

"All these human lives, all this material wealth, all this time, all this mobilization of the powers of the human race—if all this had been directed to peace, it would have had a much, much greater effect. In any case, war is no longer a profit-making business. . . . When you came back from the army, what did your officers tell you?''

" 'It's too bad! It can't be helped! Obey the Americans for the present. But just as Germany rose from the ashes of the First World War, so we too will rise again, sword in hand. Wait and be ready for that day!' That's what they said.''

"The strategems of naive people only end in disaster. Reject these ideas completely. Tell me, have these officers any experience of real war?''

"No. Their work was at home.''

"Of course. Officers who have no experience of real war! To satisfy their own vanity they shout orders to innocent youngsters and send them to the front. Real war is a cruel affair. Oh yes, it's beautiful and inspiring to lean back in an armchair and read war literature and then to reflect: 'I, too, would like to go to the front.' But the reality is different. Books describing the true face of war have been stopped by censorship. Of course there are pictures about the battles of Yoshitsune. And there are poems about General Nogi. But where is the beauty of the atom bomb? If you had been here on that day and at that time, if you had seen the hell that opened up on earth before our eyes, if you had had even a glimpse of that, you would never, never entertain the crazy thought of another war. If there is another war, atomic bombs will explode everywhere and innumerable ordinary people will be annihilated in the flash of a split second. There will be no beautiful stories, no songs, no poems, no paintings, no music, no literature, no research. Only death. Just as an anthill is crushed by a steamroller, so the whole earth will be crushed by this war. Isn't it too crazy for words?''

"You mean Japan is defeated once and for all?''

"Listen to the word of God: 'Vengeance is mine. I will repay.' God has His own way of punishing those who are unjust in His sight. Revenge is not our business.''

"Well, what is our way for the future?''

"In order to find a way I sit thinking and meditating in this little hut. But as yet I have found no answer.''

"I'd like to sit somewhere and think about this problem too.''

"Go to the mountains and meditate! If you stay in the hurly-burly of this world, you'll run around in circles without ever finding your way. You'll become the kind of person who just stamps and screams. But the blue mountains are immovable and the white clouds come and go. I look constantly at these three mountains of Mitsuyama and continue my meditation.''

With changed hearts my visitors have left me. Deep silence descends upon my hut.

I hear my five-year-old daughter Kayano talking to herself. Going outside, I find her playing the housewife with her toys. The head of a doll, some bottles, plates, the frame of a mirror are gathered together on a scorched rock. All her friends are dead.

She is chattering to herself. "Kaya-chan's house was big, wasn't it? It had an upstairs. My mom was there. She gave me bean-jam cakes to eat. I slept with a quilt. We had electricity.''

I stood there silently. Kayano kept talking about memories, one

Nagai reading to Kayano.

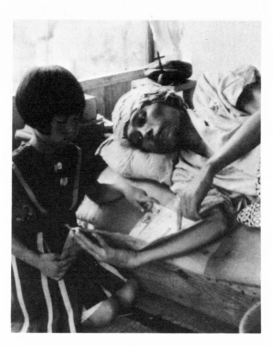

after another. As she chattered on, I closed my eyes and within me rose a vision of a life that had passed. It was like the legend of a magnificent palace at the bottom of the ocean. I opened my eyes and, like Urashima who dwelt in that palace for one hundred years, I saw my beautiful dream collapse and disappear. Before me lay nothing but an arid, atomic wasteland.

The autumn wind wailed. The tiles on the roof seemed to weep.

Suddenly Ichitaro appeared. He was wearing his military uniform with the bottom of the trousers tied around his ankles. As soon as he had been demobilized he had returned in haste, to find his city in ruins and his house a heap of ashes, while the charred, black bones of his beloved wife and five children were scattered here and there.

"I have no joy in life," he lamented.

"Who has joy when we've been defeated in war?" I replied. "I suppose you're right. Any Japanese could say what I am saying. The atomic bomb was a punishment from heaven. Those who died were evil people; those who survived received a special grace from God. But then . . . does that mean that my wife and children were evil people?"

"Well, I have a completely different view. In fact, I have the opposite view. The atomic bomb falling on Nagasaki was a great act of Divine Providence. It was a grace from God. Nagasaki must give thanks to God."

"Give thanks?"

"Look, the day after tomorrow there will be a funeral service at Urakami Cathedral for the victims of the bomb. As the representative of the Christians, I've written a speech which I intend to read there. Would you like to read it now?"

Ichitaro took the paper and began to read. At first his voice was vigorous and strong, but as he proceeded he would pause for a moment to reflect. Tears flowed down his cheeks.

Here is the text of my speech:

Funeral Address for the Victims of the Atomic Bomb

On August 9, 1945, at 10:30 A.M. a meeting of the Supreme Council of War was held at the Imperial Headquarters to decide whether Japan should capitulate or continue to wage war. At that moment the world was at a crossroads. A decision was being made that would either bring about a new and lasting peace or throw the human family into further cruel bloodshed and carnage.

And just at that same time, at two minutes past eleven in the morning, an atomic bomb exploded over our district of Urakami in Nagasaki. In an instant, eight thousand Christians were called into the hands of God, while in a few hours the fierce flames reduced to ashes this sacred territory of the East. At midnight of that same night the cathedral suddenly burst into flames and was burned to the ground. And exactly at that time in the Imperial Palace, His Majesty the Emperor made known his sacred decision to bring the war to an end.

On August 15, the Imperial Rescript which put an end to the fighting was formally promulgated, and the whole world welcomed a day of peace. This day was also the great feast of the Assumption of the Virgin Mary. It is significant to reflect that Urakami Cathedral was dedicated to her. And we must ask if this convergence of events—the ending of the war and the celebration of her feast—was merely coincidental or if there was here some mysterious providence of God.

I have heard that the second atomic bomb, calculated to deal a deadly blow to the war potential of Japan, was originally destined for another city. But since the sky over that city was covered with clouds, the American pilots found it impossible to aim at their target. Consequently, they suddenly changed their plans and decided to drop the bomb on Nagasaki, the secondary target. However, yet another hitch occurred. As the bomb fell, cloud and wind carried it slightly north of the munitions factories over which it was supposed to explode and it exploded above the cathedral.

This is what I have heard. If it is true, the American pilots did not aim at Urakami. It was the providence of God that carried the bomb to that destination.

Is there not a profound relationship between the destruction of Nagasaki and the end of the war? Nagasaki, the only holy place in all Japan—was it not chosen as a victim, a pure lamb, to be slaughtered and burned on the altar of sacrifice to expiate the sins committed by humanity in the Second World War?

The human family has inherited the sin of Adam who ate the fruit of the forbidden tree; we have inherited the sin of Cain who killed his younger brother; we have forgotten that we are children of God; we have believed in idols; we have disobeyed the law of love. Joyfully we have hated one another; joyfully we have killed one another. And now at last we have brought this great and evil war to an end. But in order to restore peace to the world it was not sufficient to repent. We had to obtain God's pardon through the offering of a great sacrifice.

Before this moment there were many opportunities to end the war. Not a few cities were totally destroyed. But these were not suitable sacrifices; nor did God accept them. Only when Nagasaki was destroyed did God accept the sacrifice. Hearing the cry of the human family, He inspired the emperor to issue the sacred decree by which the war was brought to an end.

Our church of Nagasaki kept the faith during four hundred years of persecution when religion was proscribed and the blood of martyrs flowed freely. During the war this same church never ceased to pray day and night for a lasting peace. Was it not, then, the one unblemished lamb that had to be offered on the altar of God? Thanks to the sacrifice of this lamb many millions who would otherwise have fallen victim to the ravages of war have been saved.

How noble, how splendid was that holocaust of August 9, when flames soared up from the cathedral, dispelling the darkness of war and bringing the light of peace! In the very depth of our grief we reverently saw here something beautiful, something pure, something sublime. Eight thousand people, together with their priests, burning with pure smoke, entered into eternal life. All without exception were good people whom we deeply mourn.

How happy are those people who left this world without knowing the defeat of their country! How happy are the pure lambs who rest in the bosom of God! Compared with them how miserable is the fate of us who have survived! Japan is conquered. Urakami is totally destroyed. A waste of ash and rubble lies before our eyes. We have no houses, no food, no clothes. Our fields are devastated. Only a remnant has survived. In the midst of the ruins we stand in groups of two or three looking blankly at the sky.

Why did we not die with them on that day, at that time, in this house of God? Why must we alone continue this miserable existence?

It is because we are sinners. Ah! Now indeed we are forced to see the enormity of our sins! It is because I have not made expiation for my sins that I am left behind. Those are left who were so deeply rooted in sin that they were not worthy to be offered to God.

We Japanese, a vanquished people, must now walk along a path that is full of pain and suffering. The reparations imposed by the Potsdam Declaration are a heavy burden. But this painful path along which we walk carrying our burden— is it not also the path of hope which gives to us sinners an opportunity to expiate our sins?

"Blessed are those that mourn for they shall be comforted." We must walk this way of expiation faithfully and sincerely. And as we walk in hunger and thirst, ridiculed, penalized, scourged, pouring with sweat and covered with blood, let us remember how Jesus Christ carried His cross to the hill of Calvary. He will give us courage.

"The Lord has given: the Lord has taken away. Blessed be the name of the Lord!"

Let us give thanks that Nagasaki was chosen for the sacrifice. Let us give thanks that through this sacrifice peace was given to the world and freedom of religion to Japan.

May the souls of the faithful departed, through the mercy of God, rest in peace. Amen.

Ichitaro finished reading and closed his eyes.

After a while he spoke quietly: "Then my wife and children didn't go to hell. That's for sure! . . . But, Doctor," he went on, "what about us who're left behind?''

"You and I, both of us, have failed the entrance exam to heaven!''

"We failed the exam! Ha! Ha!''

Together we raised our voices and laughed heartily. It was as though a heavy burden had fallen from our shoulders.

"I'll have to study hard,'' he said. "Otherwise I won't meet my wife and children in heaven! Those who died in war made a generous sacrifice, struggling to the end. We mustn't be outdone by them. We too must suffer.''

"Yes! Yes! We should start right away and reconstruct this atomic waste, the greatest desert in the whole world—this sorrowful, lonely, terrible desert of ash and rubble in which we now stand. We can weep with the bones of our dead, but we should struggle on.''

"I am a sinner. To suffer and expiate my sins will be a joy. Let's work and pray.''

And with a smiling face Ichitaro left me.

12

The Bells of the Atomic Waste

Immediately after the atomic explosion the theory that life could not survive in Nagasaki for seventy-five years was widely spread about. It was dangerous, people said, to return to the ruined city.

Since we had lost all our measuring instruments, the only way to find a solution to this problem was to observe the plants and animals. This we did. And after three weeks in Matsuyama, the epicenter of the bomb, we found a swarm of ants—and they were vigorous and strong. After a month we found worms in large numbers. Then we found rats running around. Insects that feed on the leaf of the potato multiplied rapidly in one month. And I began to think that if small animals could survive, human life was also possible.

As for plants, the wheat that had been exposed to the atomic blast quickly sprouted everywhere. (A year later this wheat ripened at the same time as wheat elsewhere and the grain was apparently normal.) The corn also began to sprout in winter, but it produced almost no grain. The morning glory immediately put forth vines and beautiful flowers—though the flowers were small. On the leaves, however, there were deformities. The sweet potato also immediately grew tendrils and leaves but there was almost no crop of potatoes. All types of green vegetables were good.

With this evidence I denied the theory of no-life-in-the-atomic-wilderness. I only added the warning that young children should not be brought here since they are particularly sensitive to radioactivity.

In that atomic waste the people lived through four stages of reconstruction: the stage of the dugouts, the stage of the huts, the stage of provisional houses, and the stage of constructed houses.

The first stage, immediately after the explosion, lasted for about a month. During this time, people lived in underground shelters. Sometimes they built a roof at the entrance so they could live both above and below. This could be called the stage of the refugees. It could also be called the communitarian stage because, having no houses, people gathered together in neighborhood groups and led a life in common. They worked together in dealing with the authorities and in distributing food.

In the dugouts lay many wounded people. But the few who were still strong felt a curiously deep relationship with one another. They helped one another and shared the little they had. This extremely poor existence was somehow very beautiful. It could be called the lost stage or the unconscious period. The days were spent in preparing meals and searching for the bodies of family and friends. It was a stage in which (I see when I recall it now) people were not fully conscious of what they were doing or what they would do.

From the second to the fourth month was the period of the huts. It was also a time of preparation for a new life. People had now found a reason for living. They knew the fate of their relatives and friends; they had buried their dead. They went out to the town hall; they pooled the money they had saved, and they made the first step toward reconstruction. Close relatives, brothers and sisters and cousins, got together, and, using sheet iron and scorched poles that remained after the conflagration, they built small huts about three meters square, where they could live in common.

At this time the joy and relief that they were still alive began to wear thin. The element of personal profit crept into their dealings with one another, and the smoothness of their emotional life was endangered. Close relatives, however, were able to handle these emotional problems quite easily.

But as time went on the huts could scarcely keep out the rain, nor could they protect so many people crushed into such a narrow space. In addition to this, the demobilized soldiers spread diseases like scabies.

With the fifth month it was already December. Cold winds were blowing; sleet was falling; and it became impossible to live in the huts. Carpenters and day laborers came from other parts of the city and people gave them the material with which to build. Brothers and cousins worked together and one by one they succeeded in building provisional houses. First they would build for the elder brother, and he would enter and take up residence. Next they built for his younger brother and then for all the relatives, one by one. The walls had a rough coat of plaster, and there were no ceilings— only a roof of straw. They were like modest houses in the countryside. They had tatami matting on the floor and shutters to keep out the rain. They were places where one could live in comfort.

People began to move into these houses. They began to get married; and weddings were celebrated at the rate of more than ten a week. This phase could also be called the stage of rehabilitation.

The period of final reconstruction is yet to come. It will be a period of luxury and will only be possible when Japan regains her economic and spiritual stability. At present, in spite of the rough-and-ready dwellings, residents lead a rich and happy life. Indeed, this life in provisional houses in the atomic waste is of the greatest human value.

My old professor, Dr. Suetsugi, blessed my little hut and presented me with a scroll which read:

Having nothing
Yet possessing all things.

The person who sees Urakami from the window of a train might think that it will forever be a heap of ash and debris and that resurrection is impossible. But it isn't so. Little by little, people are putting things in order and rebuilding their homes. Though it may not be apparent to the eye, the atomic desert is gradually sending forth new shoots of life. Living with deep faith and enduring courageously, this tiny group of people, who know the happiness of weeping, is suffering to make amends for the sins of the world. People without faith have not returned. Faith alone is the motivating force behind the reconstruction of Urakami.

At night, since there is no electricity, I go to bed with my children in my arms.

"How big is the atom?" asks my son Makoto who is now in the fourth grade.

"It's very, very small. If you think of it as circular in shape, then the diameter is one hundred millionth of a centimeter."

"Wow! Then we can't see it with our eyes. We can't even see

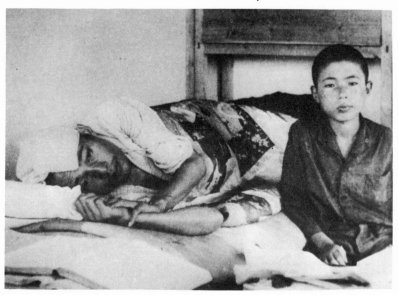

Nagai working in bed, assisted by Makoto.

it with a microscope. It's like a tiny grain, isn't it?"

"No. It isn't a grain. You've learned at school that the earth and Saturn and the other planets are constantly circling around the sun. You can imagine the immensity of the solar system from its diameter. Well, the atom isn't solid either; rather, in its center there's an atomic nucleus and, around this, negatrons are constantly revolving. The diameter of the path traversed by these negatrons is one hundred millionth of a centimeter. And between this and the atomic nucleus is nothing but empty space. The diameter of the nucleus is one hundred thousandth of the atom. It's really, really small."

"But what is this nucleus?"

"It's like the seeds inside a grape. That's what it's like. There are particles called neutrons and protons inside the nucleus. The proton has positive electricity but the neutron has no electricity."

"When the atom is split, what happens?"

"Some of the neutrons or protons are lost and in their place a terrific power is unleashed and it blows out with tremendous force. That energy can turn factories and houses into piles of rubble. And then the neutrons and the rest are blown out also. Once they penetrate the human body they cause atomic sickness."

"And the bald head of the man who makes tatami is caused by these neutrons!"

"If one atom is split it sends out a tremendous amount of energy. Since in one gram of matter there's an incalculable number of atoms, if one gram explodes, the result is terrible."

"But is there any use for atoms other than the bomb?"

"If, instead of this instantaneous explosion, we can split the atom gradually and control it—then atomic power will move ships and trains and planes. We'd have no need for coal or oil or electricity. We wouldn't need big machines. How happy the human family could be!"

"Wow! From now on everything will be done with atomic energy!"

"Yes. We're in the atomic age. Looking back in history, we see that the human race has progressively passed through the Stone Age, the Bronze Age, the Iron Age, the age of coal, the age of oil, the age of electricity, the age of radio. . . . And this year we've entered the atomic age."

"The atomic age . . . the atomic age!" Murmuring these words, the children fall asleep.

Below us the insects chirp and sing.

Will the human race be happy when it enters the atomic age? Or will it be miserable?

God concealed within the universe a precious sword. First the human race caught the scent of this awful treasure. Then it began to search for it. And finally it grasped it in its hands. What kind of dance will it perform while brandishing this two-edged sword? If we use its power well, it will bring a tremendous leap forward in human civilization; if we use it badly, we will destroy the earth. Either of these alternatives can be taken quite simply. And to turn to the left or to the right is entrusted to the free will of the human family.

The human race, with this discovery of atomic power, has now grasped the key to its future destiny—a key to survival or destruction. This is a truly awful thought. I myself believe that the only way to the proper use of this key is authentic religion.

The insects are chirping and singing. I am in bed with Kayano in my arms. She keeps groping for her mother's breasts, only to find she is with her father. She begins to sob gently. Then her breathing tells me that she has fallen into a deep sleep.

I am not alone in this suffering. Tonight in this atomic waste, how many orphans are weeping! How many widows are weeping!

The night is long but my sleep is short. My dreams fly away as the white light of the morning filters through the cracks in the shutters.

"Bong! . . . Bong! . . . Bong!"

The bells are ringing! These are the bells of the Angelus ringing out from the ruined cathedral, echoing across the atomic wilderness and telling us that dawn has come. Under the direction of Ichitaro, Iwanaga and the young men of Honno dug up those bells from beneath the atomic rubble and debris. The bells had fallen fifty meters from the cathedral tower but were not broken.

On Christmas night, Iwanaga and his companions hoisted them up and rang them morning, noon, and night until they clanged with the nostalgic sound we had often heard before.

"The angel of the Lord declared unto Mary . . ." Makoto and Kayano have jumped out of bed and, sitting on the blanket, are reciting their morning prayers.

"Bong! . . . Bong! . . . Bong!"

The clear sound of those bells!—ringing out the message of peace and its blessings. These are the bells that did not ring for weeks and months after the disaster. May there never again be a time

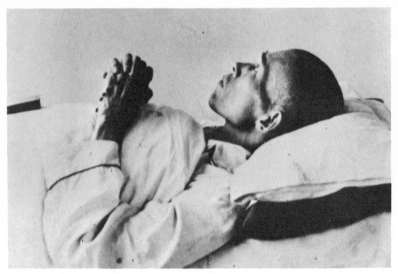

Nagai praying.

117

when they do not ring! May they ring out this message of peace until the morning of the day on which the world ends!

Men and women of the world, never again plan war! With this atomic bomb, war can only mean suicide for the human race. From this atomic waste the people of Nagasaki confront the world and cry out: No more war! Let us follow the commandment of love and work together. The people of Nagasaki prostrate themselves before God and pray: Grant that Nagasaki may be the last atomic wilderness in the history of the world.

The bells continue to ring.

"O Mary, conceived without sin, pray for us who have recourse to thee."

Makoto and Kayano make the sign of the cross as they finish their prayers.

定価2,900円
in Japan